# the turn of the century

2

# the turn of the century

# A Reader about Architecture in Europe 1990–2020

3

4

# the turn of the century

# A Reader about Architecture in Europe 1990–2020

Edited by Matthias Sauerbruch and Louisa Hutton

Lars Müller Publishers

5

6

**7**

8

9

10

Matthias Sauerbruch, Louisa Hutton

**Editorial**

We have assembled this reader to accompany our retrospective exhibition *draw love build*, which will open in September 2021 in the M9 Museum District in Mestre. Having recorded the work of our office over some thirty years in a pair of books – *archive 1* and *archive 2* (a third volume being on the way) – with drawn, written and photographed project documentations, along with explorative texts authored (without exception) by ourselves, we felt a need to anchor this reflexive practice within a broader context. Curious to hear other people's voices on subject matters that have been, and are, impacting the fields of architecture and the city during the past three decades, we asked critics, learned friends, colleagues and clients to contribute a short essay on a theme relating to the turn of the century.

This opening up came at a time when we had already decided to further formalise what we had been trying to practise over the years: a dialogic way of working – with other disciplines as well as with our own team – that had flourished as we progressed. Thirty years later, one can discern the outline of a tree whose trunk is formed by the two of us together with Juan Lucas Young. As this tree matures and develops sturdy branches, the occasion of the exhibition seemed a good moment to look back in order to go forward, and, in doing so, to have some views from outside.

We presented our request, however, independent of the office's history, as we were looking for unexpected insights and a broadening of the horizon. Naturally, though, some of the authors used either our work or personal histories as catalysts for their observations. Noting this with a degree of polite reluctance, we are obviously grateful for their shared understanding and sympathetic – as well as critical – peer reviews. In the end, the result of this experiment – which coincided with the pensive period of the pandemic – is quite an eclectic collection of thoughts that is by no means unified into a single panorama. Instead, it is a journey full of intelligence and wit, a surprising collage of individual reflections assembled during a year of evident upheaval.

Some of the texts are concerned with time: what are thirty years in terms of the larger view of things?; how do you measure this period and how can it be represented? On the one hand, three decades might span a third of an individual's lifetime (if you are lucky); they might stand for one generation (more or less); or they might represent six to eight legislatures in various governments. So, in all, thirty years is not such a long time on the scale of history. On the other, 1990 marks the first appearance of the mobile telephone on the market – the ubiquitous iPhone is today only fifteen years old. In 1990, most architects were still drawing by hand and there was no computer-aided manufacturing to speak of.

Are we unable without such indicators to notice the constant transformations of which we are part? Can an architecture be a timepiece? Can it be timeless? Both **Mark Wigley** and **Ijoma Mangold** address such questions from different angles. **Georg Vrachliotis** confronts us with certain aspects of our present time – of which we are generally still only fleetingly aware – as he takes us on an excursion into the world of artificial intelligence. Technology might already be somewhere else altogether, while architects are still struggling to establish their position as a by-product of the past. **Mohsen Mostafavi** literally writes history as he consolidates the knowledge and experience of a lifetime into a critical narrative. Looking beyond the socially, geographically and politically specific modernism of Team X via the varying reinterpretations of history in post-modernism through to deconstructivism, he sees the

**11**

profession now in a position akin to the eclecticism of the 19th century, when Heinrich Hübsch posed the question "In What Style Should We Build?" in his 1828 pamphlet of the same name. To escape such arbitrariness, **Mostafavi** advocates "a shift from image to affect", which could be achieved using the potential of space, craft and material. It is perhaps like a shift from painting to sculpture as an aesthetic frame of reference, coupled with the hope that a committed response to the "specific characteristics of a project's social, political and environmental conditions" might emerge simultaneously, almost by default.

Indeed, these concurrent developments of both general and specific cultural contexts are key reference points for us – in fact, they constitute the very condition of contemporaneity that this reader aims to address. However, as **Wigley** remarks: "The word 'architecture' might be just a name for a particular way of dancing. More precisely, it might be the name for a certain way of being out of step — more a form of syncopation than synchronisation."

In our case – as a London-Berlin-based office (which we were in the early '90s) – one of the major historic events of our time was the reunification of Germany and the associated dissolution of the East and West blocs on a macroscale and, on a microscale, the re-emergence of Berlin as the German capital. The reunification of the long-divided city and the re-establishment of a joint central government led to enormous building activity that in fact needed a leitmotif. Despite evidence of incredible enthusiasm and joy at the moment the Wall was breached, the liquidation of the once idealistically established German Democratic Republic was largely accompanied by disillusionment and a grudging admittance of failure. Deep down, there weren't many positive visions shared by both sides that could sustain this change of times beyond the aspiration to harmonise everyone's living standards to a higher level. Initial enthusiasm for freedom and democracy rather quickly gave way to political and institutional struggles between the former West and the former East, between powerful appropriation via long-standing systems and rituals and intermittent gestures of defiant independence. In architecture, the demolition of East Germany's Palace of the Republic to make way for a reconstructed Berlin Schloss amply illustrates the cultural confusion that ensued and continues to interfere with the necessary healing process today. Instead of a brave step forward into a joint future, the city withdrew into a retardant campaign of so-called Critical Reconstruction that ultimately turned "dear, fascinating, racy, sinister, sophisticated old Berlin" into "such a plodder", in the words of **Peter Cook**, who goes on to ask: "What happened to the ghosts of Poelzig, Mendelsohn and Scharoun? Why is everything so *HEAVY*?"

So this was indeed a moment in which architects were "left alone to the pragmatism of their own contingent conditions of practice", to quote Mostafavi as he speculates about post-Team X generations: the lack of a general vision offered the opportunity for individual speculation about a desirable and appropriate future. **Barry Bergdoll**, **Jean-Louis Cohen**, **Kristin Feireiss**, **Philip Ursprung** and **Dirk van den Heuvel** give eloquent testimony to various aspects of this moment, and so does **Anh-Linh Ngo** as he quotes Wolfgang Scheppe, who states that: "When the abstract principles of social, politcal and economic relations [...] are manifested in concrete form, they can be perceived viscerally and explained via these concretions. The conditions that define the production of space are thus legible in the space itself." So the evident fear of the new in urban and architectural policies can probably be read as a symptom of insecurities caused by phenomena that appeared too suddenly to be digested. The reunification exposed Germany to a greater degree of globalisation, for example – not just the former East but the Berlin Republic as a whole. On a positive level, the country in general and Berlin in particular developed into a destination for international nomads and the crowd quickly became increasingly cosmopolitan. The city started to grow, not from a surplus of births but by the sheer influx of (mostly young) people attracted by a capital in a state of becoming that rightfully proclaimed itself "poor but sexy". Of course, on a more structural level, the city and the republic also turned into objects of international finance, perhaps more than ever before.

The fate of GSW – one of our first clients – tells the story of this transition quite well. Generated in the 1930s as an association of smaller organisations committed to social and affordable housing, the company (which had been client to architects such as Mies van der Rohe, Hans Scharoun, Otto Rudolf Salvisberg and Hugo Häring, among others) grew disproportionately in the period after the war. Due to its divided status, Berlin was not a place that could develop a commercial real estate market the way West German cities did – private investment in building happened predominantly when it attracted state subsidy. So the city-owned housing associations (of which GSW was the largest) became major players in the mission to rebuild the bombed city. When we won the competition for their new headquarters in 1991, GSW already owned some 60,000 apartments and had just re-inherited another 10,000 flats that had been dispossessed by the GDR – hence the need to extend their HQ. However, only two decades later, in an effort to compensate for the mounting cost of reunification, the Berlin Senate (dominated at the time by a Socialist and Social Democratic majority) decided to sell this state-owned company to an international conglomerate of anonymous investors who, in turn, immediately started to monetise their building stock on the open market. "Our" GSW Headquarters, for example, was bought and resold by a sequence of short-term owners, with the result that it has changed hands about five times over the last decade. This provides a good illustration of how the disconnect between construction and ownership affects (the fate of) a building. What may once have been driven by an idea of common welfare becomes a pawn to the forces of the free market. Such structural change could be observed in any place that is exposed to neoliberal policies, but in Berlin it was more dramatic as the new capital emerged from a long period of paralysis induced by the Cold War. Such change obviously affected both the production and the physical nature of the city.

**Kieran Long** remembers a comparable property boom and its fateful consequences for London and goes on to describe how it currently plays out in a particularly identitarian variant in Stockholm, where the protection of the historic (image of the) inner city has become an unchallengeable priority of almost national importance. Recalling the merit that came with the *terrain vague* of the ever-incomplete Berlin – or other unresolved and potentially unprejudiced territories of any post-industrial city – he justifiably identifies these as Sauerbruch Hutton's natural habitat.

Regeneration of the various urban wastelands abandoned by faltering industries has been part and parcel of general urbanisation – another major global trend around the turn of the century. Across all continents, cities have attracted – and contintue to attract – ever-increasing numbers of inhabitants, tipping the global balance in favour of urban populations and away from those in rural areas. Now that cities have become the predominant living environment for ourselves and most of our contemporaries, city culture

**13**

has had to be reinvented as a leitmotif for recent generations. With the global shift of industrial production to Asia and with the automisation of fabrication processes in general, all accompanied by the rapid development of transport networks, a huge number of redundant infrastructures have been reinhabited to become parks, mixed-use or residential areas. Despite this momentous change of paradigm, new developments taking hold of former industrial areas typically try to perpetuate the historic *genius loci*, even though IT specialists now assume the place of former steel foundries or a museum of extra-European culture is supposed to fill the vacuum left by an abdicated monarchy.

The Architecture of the City has become a simulacrum of itself – form and content at the same time. This is also true for public space and public buildings, many of which are now under private management. Indeed, at a time when (particularly European) cities are in competition to attract tourists and when the global real estate market has become a major financial force, the built environment has turned into a portfolio of commercial assets on several levels. As a consequence, traditional cities are now strictly divided into commercially actived (expensive) historic centres and less-defined (more affordable) agglomerations that provide the necessary infrastructure – housing, production, services and education, as well as leisure and logistics, as **Ngo** describes. This infrastructural landscape often lacks visual and spatial clarity as well as human scale and orientation, so it falls to architectural interventions to provide inviting and dignified settings where little inherited building culture is to be found.

"One of the most significant tropes of late 20th- and early 21st-century urban regeneration has been that eye-popping statement buildings can serve to trigger cultural and economic rebirth in cities whose glory days are often long gone or have yet to be imagined," interjects **Veronica Simpson** critically. Nothing, however, is easy. "Faced with this situation, resisting spectacle, which in turn is merely a reaction to the generic globalised city without providing a genuine response, is the most daunting challenge for contemporary architecture," comments **Ngo**, adding that, "In the face of populist, anti-globalist tendencies," the question to which architecture, along with society as a whole, must find a response is "how we can construct an identity that is not focused on formulaic categories, but instead takes account of societal dynamics and global interconnections."

Sauerbruch Hutton's approach in these situations has been one of "inverse contextualisation", as **Cohen** describes it, with projects whose strangely supple forms, façade rhythms and colours suggest "a new reading of the pre-existing fabric within which they are placed by drawing attention to its scales, volumes and textures. The intruder does not internalise a relationship with a location's previous history, but instead articulates it by entering into a conversation with its predecessors, framed by the interstitial spaces" between the curves, by backyards, and exisiting massing – adding that "the ripples radiating outwards may encompass much more than just the surrounding buildings."

14

The Experimenta project is an eloquent example of such endeavour, firstly in the transformation of an abandoned industrial area into a productive location and secondly in its proposition of an extra-curricular place of learning. Just as the disparate yet highly sensual urban landscape – inherited from previous generations – has been reinterpreted through its experiential qualities, so these new spaces of education were conceived in the spirit of curiosity that is the fundamental driver of the institutions' playful introduction to the world of natural sciences.

**Florian Heilmeyer** traces the steps in the typological transformation of traditional schools to new rooms of learning, speculating that we are now in the process of a slow "defunctionalisation" and are looking for a new openness in architecture, for It is in the spaces in between that life, activities and encounters flourish. This observation also holds for other educational facilities such as museums. The M9 Museum District is obviously a good example of a spatial continuum in which outside and inside, public piazza and foyer, shop and learning space, display and play areas merge into and intensify one another: the building volumes and their interstitial spaces enable programmatic potential and define the qualities of place. As **Marco Biscione** writes: "Museums are no longer simply focused on preserving and displaying exhibits, but instead have become active cultural agents that aim to serve their community" – capable of making a vital contribution to local civic, cultural and economic development. Such ambition translates into spaces whose uses are not fully known when they are conceived and for this reason need to have the capacity to react to fundamental change. As a result, one of the new challenges for architecture is to create a balance between programmatic openness and clear, atmospheric determinacy. We believe that a lack of morphogenetic functionality must never lead to triviality of form, space, material or indeed colour. **Cook** and **Eric Parry** call this the "issue of delight"; we think of it in terms of love. For an environment to be sustained, it surely needs to be loved and hence loveable.

This statement may sound banal, but it provides a key transition to the overarching question that has increasingly dominated the general discussion in the last thirty years and will continue to do so: the climate crisis and how one can contribute to its deceleration. "Together, we are convinced that climate change, limited resources, global warming and the social divide have to be the key reference points in the shaping of our built environment," writes **Thomas Auer**, and these factors have indeed been driving our generation to explore a number of routes to rethink and reform the practice of architecture and urbanism. These attempts have not been in vain: in Germany, energy consumption and greenhouse gas emission in the building sector have been reduced by half, while renewable energy sources have more than doubled. However, the overall situation has not really improved – carbon dioxide emissions are steadily on the rise. In order to contain the global increase in temperature, we will have to embark on a momentous revolution that will change all aspects of our lives. Among these, the construction and maintenance of the built environment – which currently contributes 40 per cent of all emissions and 50 per cent of all global waste – still holds huge potential for improvement. The reuse and adaptation of existing housing and other stock, as well as the shift within the building industry towards low-carbon construction and the use of renewable materials, are tendencies that are gaining increasing importance.

**Angelika Fitz**'s exploration of the Care Turn describes what she sees as the necessary ethical precondition to tackle the crisis. Her reliance on a caring attitude to become the catalyst for a general turnaround may appear to be romantic and utopian in the face of today's global climate phenomena and the concurrent polarisation of democratic societies, but it is certainly a valid and long overdue appeal. **Fitz** also raises the question as to whether architects and architecture are actually still needed as the Care Turn might be delivered more effectively by activists, lawyers, planners and environmental

**15**

engineers. Being architects ourselves, we are obviously not unbiased in this matter and like to highlight the broad potential in the application of architectural knowledge and skill. Also, we firmly believe that architects care about their clients, the users of their buildings, their city and the environment at large. Nevertheless, there is scope for an extended facility management that not only includes technical and economic aspects, but is also inspired by social, spatial and aesthetic concerns. This is particularly true – at least in the European context – as existing stock represents some 75 per cent of all buildings, that is to say, new construction stands for only a fraction of the subject under consideration. But even in the context of adaptive reuse, there is still a need for architects to continually intervene in the practical and sensual world that defines our daily realities. Almost everything that surrounds us from cradle to grave can be described as architecture (of kinds), and whatever architects do (or don't do) can inspire (or not) the lives of thousands.

On the other hand, architecture as a profession or discipline has clearly been affected by the ubiquitous commodification of everything, and with this, a changing understanding of what value actually represents. As **Adrian Forty** remarks: "the greatest profits no longer accrue in quantities [...], but come rather from the capacity to create meaning." In this context, and quoting Pedro Fiori Arantes, "it has become the task of architects to provide unique and memorable experiences [...] in a form that can be mediated through an image. This expectation is very different from the modern era earlier in the 20th century, when architects were encouraged to produce universal typologies, buildings that might become a standard that could be replicated anywhere." [...] The freedom and speed with which buildings now circulate as images has led to the discovery of a new kind of value, a value unconnected to the traditional economic capacity to change land use. [...] Images of buildings now circulate so widely that those images alone have the power to bring benefits to the institutions, corporations, or individuals that own the buildings, to the cities in which they stand, and to the architects who designed them, regardless of the practical usefulness of the buildings themselves".

This must be the phenomenon to which **Mostafavi** refers when, talking about "a rebalancing between the visual and the experiential", he pleads for a shift "from image to affect". For, as **Ursprung** points out: "Like related notions such as 'surface', 'illusion', 'theatricality' and 'effect', the notion of image still has a negative connotation among most architects." However, today's predominance of the image is also a side-effect of the near exclusivity of visual media in general communication. Any pronouncement, commercial or otherwise – even the academic discourse on architecture, the ultimate three-dimensional discipline – has irreversibly been conducted in the last decades, if not century, on the basis of two-dimensional evidence. Printed documents, screens and projections have long constituted our world and shaped our imaginations – a cultural phenomenon that is also the subject of the art of **Ola Kolehmainen**, who uses the medium of photography to explore this world of images. A selection of his artworks – catalysed by some of our buildings – is presented in this reader as a visual essay. **Kolehmainen**'s works, which are usually shown in very large formats, are frequently concerned with aspects of a real space. His razor-sharp focus on form and colour lets the flat surface of his prints become almost material as a new three-dimensionality emerges that goes beyond illustrative depiction. The images assume a place in a fluctuating territory between 2D and 3D, between representation and abstraction, leaving the viewer in a state of heightened curiosity. While working with the graphic use of colour at the beginning of our collaboration, his explorations now question the image as a medium of representation even more aggressively. One could argue that, on the one hand, his work has gained more autonomy, yet on the other, it has also become increasingly narrative – both of its own making but also of a terrain that somehow exists between real life and its two-dimensional depiction.

The fact that this reader includes **Kolehmainen**'s work but no traditional architectural photography can be interpreted both as our scepticism against the all-too-simple discourse via images and, at the same time, our critical acknowledgement of the "iconic turn". In fact, for many years now, we have been searching for an architecture that oscillates between what Josef Albers would call "actual fact" and "factual fact"* – something that is aware of both effect and affect but still remains elegantly relevant, and simply intelligent for today's and tomorrow's user.

To ignore the enormous importance of the image in what Walter Benjamin called "the era of its mechanical reproduction" would be as naïve as it would be to deny the accelerating speed of its dissemination on account of digitalisation in general and the concurrent proliferation of social media in particular. **Lars Müller** describes how the role of the architectural book has changed over the last three decades: what was once a popular medium that had liberated its subject matter from its essential immobility seemed on the verge of becoming an expensive fetish in order to compete with the economy of the internet. Surprisingly, though, the book has also increasingly turned out to be a key repository of architectural ideas that would otherwise be lost. To use the term "aura" as assigned by Benjamin to the original artwork may be misleading, but critical books still have, as **Kester Rattenbury** writes, "their [...] role in sharing architectural knowledge, experience and imagination [...]. And from within such constraints, it is startling how much they can do, by assembling and curating images and text on smallish bits of paper, nicely bound together".

Just as **Müller**'s passion for architectural books was inspired and guided by Boesiger / Stonorov / Girsberger's pioneering publication project on Le Corbusier's *Oeuvre Complète*, our own work with colour and image has been fundamentally influenced by Josef Albers' thoughts on abstract painting as theorised in his seminal book *Interaction of Color*.* Our contribution to his discourse was to transfer his observations from the canvas to three-dimensional space. The result is beautifully described in **Gerhard Matzig**'s poetic essay on the colour white, where he feels reminded of the "snowstorm dream" that the main protagonist, Hans Castorp, experiences in Thomas Mann's *The Magic Mountain:* "In Mann's conception of art, which underlies this passage, art in particular transposes reality's bipolar nature from the commonplace, over-simplified concept of 'either X or Y' into the genuinely true 'both X and Y' of existence. In the famous snow scene, the realm of literary possibilities as one form amid variegated, divergent visions of life is exemplified by the snow-covered landscape, swathed in hazy white. Mann describes this *coexistentia oppositorum* as the artistic paradox."
**Matzig** continues with reference to our work: "That is precisely the aspect that has long fascinated this critic in their buildings: They can always be grasped spatially, quite literally. These are spatial universes that can be experienced through the senses and are personal, powerful and full of character. Yet colour is more than simply another dimension, for it is also the means that brings about the transformation: from seeing to feeling to touching and permeating. Spaces by this studio understood in this sense are also always spaces of possibility within the universe of *The Magic Mountain*."

**Bergdoll**'s instinct to look – in the context of colour in architecture – for a tradition of creative resistance (in direct line from Bruno Taut and Paul Scheerbart) is a sensitive reading of these attempts. **Kurt W. Forster** even sees in the use of colour a turn against "the conditions of a near-total digital regime". Further, and perhaps more importantly, we think that the issue of ecology adds a renewed dimension: the "green" movements are essentially concerned with the well-being of this and future generations, a category that is – just like health in general – dependent on both physical and psychological criteria. To provide a sustainable built environment, the task lying ahead of this generation requires on the one hand the radical reduction of emissions as well as the careful management of resources. On the other, there is a need to keep the spaces of inhabitation liveable, with atmospheres that will sustain its inhabitants through the generations. "Just as the eye and the brain are parts of the body, colour is a thing of the body first and foremost. Therefore, colour is not merely visual in your work I would suggest, it is not to be seen but to be sensed [...] to be experienced while moving around and within the building, with the light being reflected and absorbed in ever-changing ways." writes **van den Heuvel** in his touching "Letter to Berlin".

This is where architecture starts to be considered not so much in relation to its urban or cultural context but with a certain autonomy, like a work of art. As a matter of fact, art is always on our minds, much like a relative who is both loved and eyed with scepticism in equal measure for his or her irreverent, unruly and essentially liberal lifestyle. Our much-respected colleague **Parry**, for example, sees parallels with Manet and van Gogh when he looks at the work of his peers, while **Rattenbury** thinks of Bridget Riley and claims that Sauerbruch Hutton's projects are "real artworks". In our view, however, architecture is always an applied art that is mostly about the charging of space. This often requires artistic inspiration as it is certainly not enough merely to create generous room for "things to happen". Even really simple set-ups such as the living / working quarters of artist **Karin Sander** (exposed concrete on most surfaces, no colour) gain uniqueness through their proportion, light and the selection of openings and views, as well as the occasional "collaborative work". The gallery spaces in the Brandhorst Museum, which were deliberately designed to act as backgrounds to the aura of the collection, are still each specifically attuned in their various spatial qualities; individually and together, they create an intimate almost domestic environment just through light, proportion and material surface.

If this reader (and the associated exhibition) will document one overarching aspect of our work, it is the repeated attempts to understand and react to the complexities of both the physical and the cultural environments that surround us. Our cities are often confusing and not always inviting. Architecture's challenge, however, is surely to celebrate the diversity and plurality of urban life and to reduce confusion without falling into schematic simplifications. The sublimation of uncertainty into an enjoyable and empowering arrangement of three-dimensional spaces that open windows into a world of possibility is what makes architecture so enjoyable, so satisfying.

**18**

Whether or not one is successful in one's efforts is often a question of hard work and perseverance, but it is equally a matter of lucky coincidence and the help of sympathetic contemporaries: clients, colleagues of all disciplines, friends, partners in the various administrations, contractors and last, but by no means least, the growing number of team members in our own office.

No man is an island, and the moment in early 1992 – as described by **Feireiss** – when Philip Johnson and Julius Posener met Hans-Jörg Duvigneau, director of GSW, and spontaneously discussed the model of our nascent design that was being exhibited in her gallery represents one of those many, more or less important, encounters that have beaten and accompanied a path to the work on show – for which we feel some pride, but mostly gratitude.

After all the retrospection, there is finally also the (fleeting) moment of now. As **van den Heuvel** recalls, so many things have happened in the last few years – Trump, Brexit, rising nationalism, racism and xenophobia, not to mention anti-democratic tendencies and occurrences all over the world – and he rightfully asks: "How is one to drag poetry out of this brutality? How to remain optimistic?" As we continue to read on a daily basis the unbelievable numbers of Covid-related deaths and nervously await our own vaccinations, this reader is an attempt to turn the insecurity of the moment into some kind of anchor. We would therefore like to thank our authors for giving us this network into which we can tie ourselves. And we hear **Wigley** as he says: "When does an architect even become an architect? If architecture is by definition an untimely intervention, necessarily out of step with the very sense of time it brings into consciousness, what is the untimeliness that makes the architect? [...] Does a studio become a studio when it names itself, or only retroactively, when it constructs an exhibition or publication and sees itself, as it were, from the outside? Or is it when the work provokes a certain untimeliness, neither nostalgic nor futuristic but somehow lurking near the always elusive present? The work in this exhibition never strays too far from this lurking. These might be architects of our time precisely in the way they construct a hesitation around the question of the present."

Berlin, April 2021

* Josef Albers, *Interaction of Color*, 1963: XXV "On teaching color – some color terms".

20

Mark Wigley

# Time Machines

What does it mean to visit the exhibition *draw love build* in Mestre in May 2021? To visit, that is, an exhibition about the work of a Berlin-based architecture studio installed in a building designed by that studio to house a permanent exhibition of the 20th century in Italy. Celebrated for their sensitivity and inventiveness with the material experience of objects – colour, pattern, texture, light, sequence – the designers are showing a survey of their work in the first "objectless museum" in Italy. Their presentation even includes drawings and models of the very building that houses the exhibition. Or is it that the permanent building itself has become part of the temporary exhibition, turned into a kind of one-to-one model that houses all the other models made by the studio?

A confusing juxtaposition of times and spaces, then. Nothing simple there. Yet perhaps nothing more complicated than any other work of architecture. After all, buildings are always in some complex dance with the question of time. The word "architecture" might be just a name for a particular way of dancing. More precisely, it might be the name for a certain way of being out of step – more a form of syncopation than synchronisation.

Architecture is some kind of time machine. It produces senses of time and is commissioned, explained and lived in terms of such senses – as Kevin Lynch beautifully conveys in his question "What Time Is This Place?" But a time machine can never simply reside in the times it constructs or accesses. If architecture offers some kind of syncing with the present, it can do so only by being out of sync. Architecture is always in and out of time, eluding time precisely in framing it. Similarly, if architecture offers a sense of stability in our unstable worlds, it can do so only by veiling all the instabilities required to make that offer. Every seemingly simple fixed building is filled with hidden movements and convoluted geometries. Architecture's relationship to space and time is never straightforward. Buildings are choreographed assemblies of fixed straight lines but are never straight or static.

Take the recently completed M9 Museum in the neighbourhood in which this exhibition is taking place. It is more urban fabric than building. The architects have reinforced the historical context of a diverse mixture of buildings, adding ways of moving through the site and sequences of public spaces, only to make a larger, clearly differentiated object appear within those spaces. Its mass, dramatic angles and coloured pattern of ceramic tiles seem to support a horizontal exposed concrete volume that has a jagged roof pattern reminiscent of a factory – as if the new object were rising up from below the ground and pushing the industrial volume up into the air. And yet at its heart, this sharply defined colourful object has an absence of form, texture, colour and light. Like some kind of exotic fruit, the object wraps itself around a buried kernel, two floors of media space for presenting the previous century, in which the buildings of the present have given way to electronic constructions of the past. These dark spaces hosting "all-digital" interfaces are hidden behind the brightly coloured tiles of the façade. They are sandwiched between the partially exposed temporary gallery space above and the partially exposed auditorium below. In other words, to go to the heart of the building is actually to leave the building and the 21st century behind.

The project thus constructs a kind of convoluted archaeology of time, with the outer parts of the site linked to the 19th-century industrial past, the central building to the 21st century, and the core of that building to the 20th century. In other words, the 20th century lurks within the 21st century, which has just emerged out of the 19th century. The passage through fabric, object and emptiness is a kind of time travel – or at least a journey that is at once spatial and temporal. But common to each of these folded layers of space and time is the seemingly simple thought that architecture could, should and does present time. Which is not so straightforward if you think about it. Imagine an object, outfit, expression or protocol that is perfectly synchronised with the time in which it was made, worn, seen, read or enacted. Would it not be, by definition, invisible, immersed in the flow of its own time, indistinguishable from all the other symptoms of the present? One might be able to single it out only retroactively, as uniquely capturing that time, but even then, only if it were different from other possible representatives. Paradoxically, the thing that represents a time cannot ever be simply of that time. The very idea of creating an object "of its own time" is tricky. The things that most capture a time are perhaps the ones that do not fit in, or those that disturb the present, and are therefore memorable for that very reason and give us a sense of what it is that they stand out from. A certain lack of synchronisation exposes or even manufactures a sense of the present.

And yet so much discourse around architecture is orchestrated by the ambition or demand that buildings should faithfully represent "their" time. Think of "modern architecture", the expression most often used to describe the architecture identified with the 20th century. It implies an object that is uniquely of its time – modern in the sense of timely. When Otto Wagner first used the expression as the title of an architectural manifesto in 1895, the whole point of his book was that architecture had to carry "the stamp of its own time" – a point that had already been made for decades by a succession of protomodern architects and endlessly repeated by others in subsequent decades. Architects are supposed to come to terms with the present, and their responsibility is both to represent that present and offer ways for people to adjust to it and live within it. In a sense, the present is treated as the real architect.

Take Le Corbusier's 1924 introduction to *Towards an Architecture*, arguably the single most influential manifesto for modern architecture. Architecture is not produced by designers but by shifts in collective thinking:

"To do architecture! This is not just a matter of the technical work of professionals. It is characteristic changes of direction, impulsive movements of the shared idea, that demonstrate in what mode it means to organise its acts.

Thus does architecture become a mirror of the times."

Architectural discourse in the 20th century was filled with claims about the 20th-century mentality. Every "modern" architect or architectural theorist acted as a historian, telling a story about what used to happen in contrast to what happens now. Other architects are routinely chastised for being out of touch with the present and needing to catch up. Manifestos for modern architecture were not calls to develop a new architecture but to embrace the forms, technologies, media and methods that had already arrived. Indeed, the central argument of the most influential modern architects (like Le Corbusier) and the most influential historians of modern architecture (like Sigfried Giedion) was that a new architecture of industrialisation had arrived in the mid-19th century and that architects needed to finally embrace it. The radical architecture of the 1920s was the one that finally channelled the innovations in industrialisation of the 1830s to 1850s. As Giedion put it in his first book on modern architecture in 1928 (*Bauen in Frankreich, Bauen in Eisen, Bauen in Eisenbeton* – Building in France, Building in Iron, Building in Ferroconcrete): "the architecture we now describe as 'new' is a legitimate part of an entire century of development." Indeed, the 20th century "scarcely has the right" to compare itself to the "bold" advances of the 19th century.

22

The discourse around modern architecture was not just about new times but new senses of time. Giedion's pioneering and influential history *Space, Time and Architecture* (1941) was nothing more than this argument, offering a history of concepts of time and architecture's intimate relationship to them. The book begins by echoing the opening line of his 1928 book, which insisted that, like artists and architects, "Even the historian stands within, not above, time." *Space, Time and Architecture* repeats that historians need to be "in close contact" with the present: "only when he is permeated by the spirit of his own time is he prepared to detect those tracts of the past which previous generations have overlooked." Furthermore, it is "modern" artists who have shown Giedion how fragments "lifted from the life of a period can reveal its habits and feelings". The capacity of a contemporary art object to bring the hidden state of the present to the surface acts as the model for exposing the hidden state of the past.

This very idea of a timely analysis and a timely architecture implies, of course, an environment that is untimely or appears so. Giedion's model is psycho-analysis. The truth of present is never simply present and the role of both artist-architects and historians is to bring repressed truths to the surface. As a student of Heinrich Wölfflin, Giedion was very familiar with the way Hegel had famously rethought Herder's idea of the *Zeitgeist* (the spirit of the times) by arguing for the need to actively resist the present in order not to be asphyxiated by it, and he was also aware of Friedrich Nietzsche's role as the very prophet of the "untimely". The generic call for architecture to synchron-ise with the present is actually a call for furniture, buildings and cities to engage with the untimely and even to act in seemingly untimely ways to lure the present into consciousness. Again, architecture cannot simply partici-pate in or embody the sense of time it constructs or presents. But neither is it simply outside that time. Like the frame of a painting, it is both inside and outside what it frames – an outside folded into the inside and vice versa – in order to act as a form of hospitality to a sense of time. A genuinely modern architecture is therefore not the architecture that looks modern or even the one that deploys modern materials and means, but the architecture that brings a sense of the present into consciousness. Modernity is a state of mind that has to be hosted by something that cannot itself be simply modern.

A 20th-century architecture is therefore not the one made during the years from 1900 to 2000, but one that hosts a particular state of mind. A 20th-century architecture might well appear in the following century, or even in the previous one. The whole question of when a century really begins is per-manently up in the air – as is the question of when it is that an architecture starts to present it, or when that presentation eventually becomes a detach-ment rather than engagement with the present.

This enigma is eloquently framed by the title of this reader, *The Turn of the Century*, edited by the founders of an architectural office formed in the 20th century to accompany an exhibition of that practice's work taking place in the 21st century in a museum of the 20th century. It is worth recalling that Le Corbusier's very last and uncompleted project, in 1965, was for a "Museum of the 20th Century", commissioned by André Malraux, who in 1947 had already described the inevitable displacement of the traditional museum by new media. More precisely, he described the outdating of traditional mu-seums in the face of the "musée imaginaire", the museums we each carry in our heads – which is not the "museum without walls" as normally translated, but the personal mental museum, a new kind of private collection reinforced by seemingly placeless or spaceless media, such as photography and television. Malraux was documenting what was already happening, not prophesising what was about to happen. In fact, for museums, the challenge posed by contemporary digital technology long preceded the digital age. The notion of an electronic museum is even contemporary with the idea of modern architecture, although it is not yet fully channelled by today's architects.

This raises a more fundamental question – one that comes before when and how architects present a sense of time – namely when does an architect even become an architect? If architecture is by definition an untimely intervention, necessarily out of step with the very sense of time it brings into consciousness, what is the untimeliness that makes the architect? For all the obsession with timeliness in architectural discourse, architects, and what they design, can never simply be creatures of their own time. Does a studio become a studio when it names itself, or only retroactively, when it puts together an exhibition or publication and sees itself from the outside, so to speak? Or is it when the work provokes a certain untimeliness, neither nostalgic nor futuristic but somehow lurking near the ever-elusive present?

The work in this exhibition never strays too far from this lurking, and these architects may be of our time precisely in the way they construct a hesitation around the question of the present. It is as if the studio relishes operating in places where things are not quite working, neglected, seemingly misfits or regarded as ugly. Their work is not to repair, heal or smooth over, but to magnify the disconnects and contradictions into new forms of interaction – preserving, as it were, the apparent untimeliness and raising the question of whether it might be timely after all. Traumatised, uncertain, inequitable, unsustainable cities are tweaked. Optimism is hosted where it is least expected.

Following Giedion's way of thinking, not only does each generation of architects have to help bring into consciousness a different present to their fellow citizens who already see things with different eyes, but the discipline of architecture itself has to catch up by seeing itself and acting differently. This exhibition is not so much about the kind of work that a particular architectural studio produces as it is about the new kind of thoughtful studio produced by that work.

Ijoma Mangold

# On Time Passing

The longer I think about these two dates, 1990 and 2020, the clearer it seems to me what I need to write about: architect envy. *Genetivus obiectivus*, that is to say, about my envy of architects. And that has something to do with this profession's connection to the phenomenon of the new: architects construct something new; this is simply what they do.

Yet the new poses a complex challenge to our psychological perceptual apparatus and generally proves impossible for us to imagine, for initially, the new does not appear as tomorrow's triumphant superpower whose fate we would be well advised to link to our own, but instead emerges as a fluctuating uncertainty, a questionable discrepancy and bizarre eccentricity that we would be wise to keep at a distance. Only when the new has already gained the upper hand do we realise that something has changed permanently. We fail to grasp the new until it has already become established.

This mindset is no surprise to anyone familiar with the stock markets. With hindsight, how many of us now wish we had acquired a stake in Amazon or Apple when their shares were still affordable? But that is easy to say ten years later, once it has become clear that Apple and Amazon are indeed the new defining phenomena. Even if their ascent seems to have been inevitable in retrospect, it was nonetheless an uncertain, multifaceted and bewildering process while it was still unfolding.

The world has always undergone change, ever since the advent of historical time, but most people would agree that the pace of such change has now become utterly frenetic. Yet here, too, it is not at all straightforward to be a witness to such transformations. Perceiving change is akin to sensing motion: provided the vehicle we are in has good suspension and decent shock absorbers, we scarcely notice that we are moving. Only when the vehicle begins to accelerate or its brakes go on do we realise how fast we have been moving – thanks to inertia, curiously enough. Afterwards, we may well be amazed to see how far we have travelled. It is exactly the same with our sense of historical movement: we hardly notice that everything is changing until we look back, astonished to realise that nothing is how it used to be.

The two epoch-defining caesurae of 1990 and 2020 remind us particularly vividly of that experience. These are also significant dates in my own biography, as 1990 marked the start of my adult life, in other words, the period when we are responsible for perceiving, reading and interpreting the signs of the times.

1990–2020. What kind of account can be given of these three decades?

The collapse and disintegration of the East bloc and the end of the Cold War – both of which had seemed likely to go on for ever – mark the beginning of this "epoch", which has come to an end with a pandemic that the German chancellor has described as the worst thing to happen since the Second World War. It would therefore be fair to say that quite a lot has happened. And yet, surprisingly, at least in the over-satiated West, the prevailing mood is generally one of stagnation: that nothing has changed; everything is coated with mildew; there are no longer any utopias or radical visions, merely a tedious perpetuation of the status quo, the stolid administration of a familiar setting. Academic circles even came up with a boastful term to describe this attitude towards life. There was talk of living in "post-history", which is to say a state of affairs in which history no longer moves determinedly in a particular direction with the aggressive vigour of the arrow of progress.

It was actually a remarkable process: the Iron Curtain was lifted, Eastern Europe was set free to enjoy liberty and self-determination, and in the wake of brief but euphoric firework displays and Beethoven's "Ode to Joy", contemporaries felt that they were living in a boring era devoid of decisive events. At the time, American philosopher Francis Fukuyama talked about the end of history, yet the flood of dramatic events actually never stopped. A blood-soaked civil war in former Yugoslavia, the advent of digitisation, the attacks of 9/11, the 2008 financial crisis – the fonts in the headlines grew larger and larger, the pace of breaking news shot up, crisis after crisis was proclaimed, yet in the West, the general public suffered from ennui and a feeling of stagnation. We are probably like drug addicts when it comes to historical experiences: we need ever-higher doses of dramatic events, for otherwise we no longer feel any effect.

It was not until Donald Trump was elected president of the United States in 2016 that everyone suddenly had a queasy feeling that something had indeed happened, that events had even spiralled out of control, because no one had asked for this kind of historical change. By comparison, the previously much-maligned status quo and stagnation had actually been quite comfortable. It was only when Trump attacked NATO that we realised just how important it was to us, and only when he put the proposed TTIP trade agreement on ice that we realised that free trade might be worth defending after all. In other words, the historical transformation did not become apparent to us until we were deprived of something we had previously taken for granted and had more or less ignored. That, in a sense, is a negative awareness of the new.

In Shakespeare's tragedy *King Lear*, Edward proclaims towards its conclusion: "We that are young / Shall never see so much, nor live so long." This sums up an experience each generation encounters anew: the feeling of having already left behind major historical developments, while the present has settled into a somewhat dreary mediocrity. And although Hamlet still says of his father: "He was a man, take him for all in all / I shall not look upon his like again," it is actually Hamlet himself who is about to surpass his father in terms of his (cultural-)historical impact.

Younger people's historical envy towards previous generations is a specific form of blindness that deprives them of the best that the present offers each generation by way of amazing novelties. Back in my youth, in the 1990s, I also viewed post-modernism as being a toned-down realm in which nothing much ever happened. I was convinced that the more exciting dramas were all a thing of the past and consigned to the history books. Could I have been any more mistaken?

In the next step, rigorous self-assessment cannot be avoided: are we actually missing the decisive aspect if we always view the present in which we live merely as a continuation of what is old and familiar rather than perceiving it as a fermenting mass, bubbling away energetically and permanently generating the new? How often have I been annoyed with myself for not being faster to spot a new phenomenon and so become its early commentator and interpreter? Are there perhaps places other than good old Europe where it is easier to recognise the new?

**27**

At this point, I should like to return to my envy of architects. I have always had the feeling that architects have an edge on the rest of us. After all, they are always obliged to build something new; if they don't embrace the new, there is little point in their even getting out of bed in the morning. That, I enviously imagine, may be why they are so much more aware of how many new things – surprisingly and incredibly new things – are happening all the time in this world. Architecture is certainly an international profession. Architects, I think to myself, operate outside this mildewy bubble of the West, where everyone feels they are riding off into a long sunset of decline.

Then I think of a city like Singapore, an architectural city par excellence, where impatient eagerness for the future leaps out at you from every street corner. Rather than fretting over apocalyptic worries, people there seem happy every morning when the sun rises, because they cannot wait to build an even more beautiful, futuristic skyscraper (complete with hanging gardens). My envy of architects is also an envy of Asia, for I, too, would like to work in a profession whose output and skills are in demand in megacities in the Far East. Unfortunately, that will never be the case for a German journalist, and it is why this particular German journalist only ever encounters people who feel that nothing is happening any longer and are convinced that everything is in a logjam and making no headway at all.

Although architecture, as a technology-driven industry, is automatically in league with the future, it also creates something new that will, at best, last far longer than most other human achievements. Creating something new that will endure – isn't that the greatest feeling of all?

The question of the new and technology are directly linked. Technological innovations always exude disruptive force. While such innovations have, throughout human history, been responsible for almost every aspect of the comfort and standard of living we enjoy today, I have the impression that attitudes towards technological progress range from scepticism to hostility, at least in Western societies. Technology is viewed as a machine that generates soulless environments that alienate people from each other and may in the end even render them superfluous, the worst-case scenario being one in which robots seize power and colonise our consciousnesses. It is no coincidence that science fiction is predominantly a dystopian literary genre. As artificial intelligence gradually begins to give our sluggish brains a helping hand in more and more ways, we become increasingly attached to our frailty, as if fallibility and weakness constitute the quintessence of human nature, as if our true charm lay in being so antiquated.

My envy of architects may be leading me astray with too much romantic glorification: but doesn't architecture embrace this tension or polarity? It draws on and deploys all the technological innovations it can find; it turns the surface of the world inside-out and gives it a futuristic twist, which, in the best-case scenario, does not involve submerging people under concrete, but instead creates liveable spaces that offer freedom. Architecture conceives spaces for a future in which nothing remains as it once was, yet where we nonetheless find a new home. It is, in effect, condemned to remain optimistic about the future – for architects who are pessimistic about our culture can only reconstruct the past.

**28**

That means that when I look at these two dates, 1990 and 2020, I begin to feel a certain gratitude for all these events: a great deal more has happened than I first thought. And then I hope that my retrospective insight into this plethora of changes may possibly sharpen my gaze for the probably equally enormous changes the next decade holds in store for us. Perhaps this time I shall be somewhat faster to recognise what is new!

Georg Vrachliotis

# Architecture, Nature and Data

"Whatever the building type, we pursue a sensitive and inventive dialogue between nature and architecture. We believe in a sustainable yet progressive approach to architecture, seeking at all times to create rewarding projects for our partners and clients." These lines are a personal statement. They refer to individual convictions and belief in a particular attitude, to the relationship with one's clients and an inventive dialogue between architecture and nature. The two sentences sum up Sauerbruch Hutton's architectural self-image. They sound like a quotation and might easily have come from an interview or one of their many lectures, and yet, as authentic and personal these words may sound, this statement never really existed. Anyone who thinks they are hearing Louisa Hutton and Matthias Sauerbruch will be disappointed. For those lines come neither from the architects nor from any member of their team. Strictly speaking, they were not even produced by a human being, but by the Generative Pre-Trained Transformer language software, known as GPT-3 for short. The programme is the third generation of an artificial intelligence that is considered one of the most impressive products our digital culture has so far created. GPT-3 is a text generator that can write poems and dramas, give answers to complex questions on topics like love or trust, discuss the weather or international climate change policy with us – it also wrote the above statement about Sauerbruch Hutton. *The New York Times* calls the programme "amazing, spooky, humbling and more than a little terrifying".[1]

## In search of modern humans

"Modern humans want and need to use technology to become independent and highly mobile within the loose framework of a social order. A supply of ready-made goods along with periodically changing habits and tools make this easier for them,"[2] proclaimed Yona Friedman in 1957, in the process rewriting a core conceptual idea in architecture's long and ongoing quest to grasp an image of modern humanity. The response proposed by Friedman and many of his contemporaries is now familiar: they believed that systems of stackable furniture for the home, built from inexpensive materials, offered a fitting architectonic concept for a society of the future that would be shaped by industrialisation, communication media and mobility. You might say that their dream entailed organising the spatial and technical aspects of social communication processes in pursuit of the utopian aspiration to develop something akin to a built anthropology. However, the traits that might constitute what is dubbed the modern individual remained unclear.

Almost at the same time as Friedman's proposal, two philosophers of technology, Abraham Moles and Herman Grégoire, were also dealing with this question, as is chronicled in the final volume of the ten-volume *Enzyklopädie des technischen Jahrhunderts* (Encyclopaedia of the Technical Century).[3] In contrast to Friedman, though, Moles and Grégoire thought on a considerably larger scale. Given increasing global networking based on information technology, they held that the human individual had evolved into a "citizen of the world" and was thus now actually something "completely new". For Moles and Grégoire, this conversely signified that the concept of "humanity" – and this aspect is particularly remarkable from today's perspective – was essentially a genuine "technological discovery". Although this sounds like a deterministic idea, conceptually, it is not so far removed from the thought collectives with whom we are familiar from Silicon Valley. Don't we need the intellectual vanishing point of technology in order to understand the entire social and political dimension of human beings from this perspective? Haven't humans always largely defined themselves through the culture of their technical advances and thus also through architecture? These are tricky questions. Moles and Grégoire, at any rate, had a clear opinion on this point. In their view, architects still produced dwellings that were nothing more than "defence lines of the past". They argued that people lead lives "not adapted and appropriate to the present". The remarkable thing about this sweeping statement is not its clear critique of post-war modernist architecture, but rather the way in which it establishes an early theoretical link between architecture, cosmopolitanism and information technology. Nowadays, we are deeply immersed in a powerful digital web that would be virtually impossible to unravel. All the more reason to ask: what kind of life would be appropriate to the present? And what has actually become of the search for modern humans?

## The world as a database

The foundations of the modern World Wide Web were laid at the European Organization for Nuclear Research (CERN)[4] in 1989, the year the Berlin Wall came down. Computer scientist Tim Berners-Lee helped to craft the first websites and the ground-breaking concept of hyperlinks. Television viewers were shown images of cheering crowds. Both these developments altered our view of architectural, urban and social space, leading not least to the questioning and radical expansion of traditional notions of "public" and "information".[5] The focus was no longer on shattering an intellectually rigid society living under the shadow of National Socialism, as had still been the case in the mid-20th century. Nor was it about the conscious fusion of aesthetics and life, so vehemently demanded by artistic avant-garde movements. Instead, the issue suddenly up for debate was a new system of coordinates in which to find one's political bearings – set between geopolitical détente on the one hand and technological networking on the other.

That is why sociologist Manuel Castells also described the "turn of the century" as the beginning of what could be called the network society[6] and thus coined perhaps one of the most influential contemporary descriptions of the last decades.

Since then, we have seen once hefty computing machines lose weight, yet gain power. The miniaturisation of technology has led to sensors populating our environment and creating their own intelligent ecosystems. As a result, the very meaning of technology has shifted – turning away from an object-oriented and mechanical meaning towards what one might perhaps call the "open machine", that is to say, complex technical assemblages of human and non-human entities that are almost, if not entirely, impossible to grasp with traditional understandings of technology as an instrument. In the form of theories put into practice, far removed from the visible realm, computer codes enter into a novel and potent connection with machines: content that is transmitted to thousands of computers, copied, and becomes part of our everyday world through constant repetition is self-stabilising and ultimately becomes a "cultural sediment of the system".[7] Computers are not simply passive vectors for signs, they actively generate them – signs produce signs. The world becomes a world in database form. What we will remember in the future, and in what form, has therefore long depended on who organises and controls the storage media and which medium serves to pass on our experiences. The very concept of storage has become synonymous with automated accumulation and evaluation of the enormous amount of data we produce. Fragments of information are continually generated, stored, retrieved, updated and stored again – a seemingly endless cycle of globalised encoding and recoding of history and the present. It is as if we lived in our own archive. But what does it mean to design within such an archive?

## Towards a new ecological design thinking

The continuous datafication of the world demonstrates to us what it means to be part of a globally operating industrial complex. This is especially true for architectural production.[8] Materials, objects and capital circulate in an infrastructural matrix whose scale and impact we are only gradually beginning to perceive clearly. Thanks to more precise simulation models for cycles of processed and unprocessed materials, we are increasingly able to document and research the consequences of an environment completely transformed by humans. Emerging digital mappings spark new insights and at the same time call traditional supply and production systems into question. We are only slowly realising, for example, that the way in which buildings are produced and constructed around the world no longer involves only our planet's surface, but also leaves traces deep inside the Earth. Laborious processes are deployed to mine and process sandstone, iron, copper or lithium for the global construction industry. Even the ocean has been transformed from a once mythical locus into a vast geopolitical infrastructure project whose history now encompasses oil platforms, submarine cables, floating server farms and forensic oceanography. How will we be able to conceptualise construction, raw materials and digitisation in conjunction with one another? And what kind of geological footprint will actually be left by future data-based digital production of architecture? These thorny yet important issues are not concerned just with innovation, but are also about responsibility and will certainly shape building in decades to come to a much greater degree than we suspect. It will be crucial to develop concepts for data-ecological design thinking for the 21st century.

## Nature, data and architecture – a new dialogue

An open society is viewed as one of the most significant civil society projects we have inherited from the last century. The significance of this legacy for the future lies in our collective responsibility to constantly question and renegotiate the concept of "openness". Depending on the context in which we talk about an open society, ideas about it change as well. It makes a difference whether it signifies, for example, the political foundations of a democracy, the economic principle underpinning a market economy or how personal data is handled. At present, there is much talk of what is referred to as an Open Data Society, in which data would be treated as a public good for the benefit of every member of the community. In that kind of future, architects would also have access to all current data about our built and natural environment, for example statistics on the worldwide consumption of sand, formation of microplastics in oceans and groundwater, the toxic properties of certain building materials or the behavioural patterns of city dwellers. The cultural technique of design would simultaneously command new media, technical, environmental and political foundations on a planetary scale. Although this is still a thought experiment, it clearly indicates the direction that architecture might pursue. Dreaming of a proposed Open Data Society is one side of the coin. The flipside is the question as to how one can design sustainably in such a data society, and how one can produce meaning from vast quantities of environmental data. For that reason alone, we shall not be able to avoid implementing novel tools – such as machine learning – in architecture in the future, as human intuition will reach its natural limits in the face of such enormous data volumes. We are collecting ever more data on materials, the environment and the climate. Yet the more rapidly this information is collected, the more likely we are to run up against the limitations of our own judgement. The issue could be described as interpretative sovereignty over the built and natural environment. We shall have to admit that we will not be able to either evaluate or judge the complex structure of an Open Data Society without automated analytical capabilities. It therefore appears that we are on the horns of a new technological dilemma.

"Architecture, more than almost any other cultural medium, is always an expression of its time," as Louisa Hutton and Matthias Sauerbruch stated in their lecture "What Does Sustainability Look Like?" – reflecting classical modernism's intellectual credo that the present should form the starting point for our thoughts and actions.[9] Yet what does that mean in an era in which architecture faces the enormous challenge of attempting to strike a balance between climate change and artificial intelligence? French philosopher Cornelius Castoriadis, for example, asserts in *The Imaginary Institution of Society* that "It is impossible to understand what human history has been or what it is now outside of the category of the imaginary. No other category permits us to reflect on these questions."[10] A sympathetic and wise assertion that gets to the heart of Louisa Hutton and Matthias Sauerbruch's conception of their design identity: the idea that, in architecture, we are constantly searching for new models of how to live together and for spaces of community – socially, politically, aesthetically and in technical terms, too. One of the most fundamental questions for architecture in the 21st century will be how we manage to reconceptualise the dialogue between nature and architecture with data as a foundation.

1   Farhad Manjoo, "How Do You Know a Human Wrote This?", *The New York Times*, 29 July 2020, https://www.nytimes.com/2020/07/29/opinion/gpt-3-ai-automation.html (accessed 2 March 2021).

2   Friedman, Yona, "Ein Architektur-Versuch", in *Bauwelt*, 16 (April 1957): 361–63.

3   Herman Grégoire and Abraham Moles, "Das Bild des modernen Menschen", in *Epoche Atom und Automation. Enzyklopädie des technischen Jahrhunderts*, ed. Ludwig Albert, vol. 10 (Geneva 1959), pp. 75 ff.

4   See Tim Berners-Lee, "Information Management: A Proposal" – a document written in March 1989 and distributed by Berners-Lee to his colleagues at CERN in May 1990.

5   See Jan Wenzel (ed.), *Das Jahr 1990 freilegen* (Spector Books, 2020).

6   Manuel Castells, *The Rise of the Network Society, The Information Age: Economy, Society and Culture*, vol. I (Malden, Mass./Oxford, UK: Blackwell, 1996).

7   Georg Trogemann, "Code and Maschine", in Andrea Gleiniger and Georg Vrachliotis (eds.), *Code. Between Operation and Narration, in the book series Context Architecture. Architectural Concepts between Art, Science and Technology* (Basel, 2010), p. 41.

8   "We find ourselves at the end of industrial society, and we have, justifiably, a far more critical relationship to technology and progress than was the case at the beginning of the twentieth century. We no longer operate against the background of a more or less active bourgeois society, but in an environment that is increasingly fragmented in social terms as well. Furthermore – and perhaps most dramatically – we are confronted by climate change and by a dwindling supply of natural resources." From a lecture by Matthias Sauerbruch, delivered in July 2002 at the UIA World Congress of Architects. Full text published as "Modernity without Dogma" in *Sauerbruch Hutton. Archive* (Baden: Lars Müller Publishers, 2006), pp. 94–103.

9   "What Does Sustainability Look Like?", in *Sauerbruch Hutton. Archive* (Baden: Lars Müller Publishers, 2006), pp. 272–77, here p. 273.

10   Cornelius Castoriadis, *The Imaginary Institution of Society* (Cambridge, Mass.: MIT Press, 1987), p. 160.

Mohsen Mostafavi

# 34 Architecture and the Burden of Influence

"Poets and prophets, like magicians, learn their craft from predecessors. And just as magicians will invoke the real or supposed source of an illusion as part of the patter, or distraction from what his hands are doing, the most ambitious poets also take some stance about sources in the past, perhaps for an analogous purpose."

John Hollander, 1973

If the first part of the 20th century was marked by experiments in integrated pedagogy (Bauhaus) and new forms of living – urbanism and habitat (CIAM) – much of what took place in the second part of the century was in reaction to those experiments. In particular, the formation of Team X and its rethinking of many of the tenets of modernism culminated in the development of an architecture more attuned to social, political and geographical specificity.

The end of the 20th century coincided with the passing of many of the figures at the core of Team X, and the story of the group – despite the attention paid to its key figures, Alison and Peter Smithson – remains incomplete, especially with regard to the contributions of its less well-known members. Still, in the context of urbanisation and the discussions surrounding globalisation, Team X's call for a socially diverse, human-centred, neighbourhood-based approach towards the planning of cities remains relevant today – even if they themselves did not always respond to that call with the same degree of sensibility they either hoped for or invoked. Robin Hood Gardens, with its "streets in the air", was the Smithsons' only large-scale housing project to reach fruition. The recent and unfortunate demolition of this iconic work, less than fifty years after its completion, draws a line under the era of optimism about the possibility of a "heroic" response to the question of housing.

Despite its idiosyncratic character as a movement, Team X events were a place of lively encounters. Their meetings resulted in serious discussions about the status of architecture in different parts of the world. Apart from the core members of the group, they involved a geographically diverse range of participants, with invitations extended to figures such as Louis Kahn and Kenzo Tange, among others. Peter Smithson, in turn, participated in the World Design Conference in Tokyo in 1960, which promoted the founding of the Metabolist group in Japan. Later, there would be other visionary groups, such as Archigram, Superstudio and Archizoom, each with its own imaginary propositions for the future of design and the social world.

Since that time, with the demise of CIAM, Team X and other groups, there has not been the same impulse – or the same physical platforms – for an international collective dialogue between architects. But does the end of these events signal a crisis of ideas for architecture and its role in society today? Or is architecture better off without such movements and their manifestos, with each architect or firm left alone to the pragmatism of their own contingent conditions of practice? Today, we are not only the inheritors of such conflictual questions, but also the bearers of the task of working our way through them. Hence the need for not only pragmatic action, but also historical and theoretical reflections.

Pancho Guedes, the Mozambique-based Portuguese architect, was a member of Team X, and through him, European architects became acquainted with the possibilities of an architecture in dialogue both with local traditions and art. His approach in part involved a continuation of an earlier strand of European modernism in Africa championed by figures such as Maxwell Fry and Jane Drew. But in addition to the role of climate, which gave rise to elements such as screens and perforated façades for shading in the "tropical modernism" of Fry and Drew, Guedes' architecture was more directly inflected by local, African cultural conditions. At times reminiscent of the early buildings of Oscar Niemeyer, his work took on board the topic of ornament. By embracing the role and comparative freedom of the artist, he was able to overcome some of architecture's disciplinary orthodoxies and produce a body of work that combined colour, locality, geometry, modernity, structure and emotion.

The Smithsons had a close connection with artistic practice as well, but their collaboration with their Independent Group partners, the sculptor Eduardo Paolozzi and the photographer Nigel Henderson, was primarily focused on intellectual topics such as the "as found". This linked their pro-jects to the anthropology of everyday life and gave them a certain untreated quality, a material rawness, which nevertheless produced its own material and poetic qualities. While these are characteristics shared with the "art brut" of Jean Dubuffet, their efforts appear at times to lack "the solitude ... and the pure and creative impulses" which Dubuffet had advocated as a precondition of "art brut" and which Guedes more generally associated with the freedom of the artist. It was only towards the end of their careers that the Smithsons embraced a more artistic and colourful approach in their work for the German furniture manufacturer Axel Bruchhäuser and his company, Tecta.

Apart from Guedes and fellow Team X member Aldo van Eyck, who experi-mented with the concept of "play" through his hundreds of urban playgrounds built around Amsterdam after the Second World War, the world of architec-ture increasingly shifted away from art and towards a greater awareness of history as a means to interpret and conceive buildings. Yet there was no unified or singular attitude towards history among architects. The differing treatments of the topic would range from Aldo Rossi's *L'architettura della città* to Robert Venturi's *Complexity and Contradiction in Architecture,* both published in 1966. They remain relevant documents for our contemporary debates on architecture and urbanism.

In these books, and in the work of others, the "monument" was the protag-onist, the lens through which the connections with the past were examined. Sert, Léger and Giedion published a short manifesto with the title "Nine Points on Monumentality" in 1943. Louis Kahn's articulation of "new monu-mentality" as a spiritual quality, from as early as 1944, would become the means by which he both conceived of a public architecture and, simultan-eously, established its links to history. Venturi's own explorations oscillated from the careful and abstract demonstrations of the Vanna Venturi House (1964), or the Fire Station no. 4 in Columbus, Ohio (1968), to the more explicitly mannerist and flattened treatment of historical motifs in the Sains-bury Wing extension of the National Gallery (1991), the latter two projects undertaken with his partner, Denise Scott Brown.

The struggle for the recovery of history in architecture was exemplified not only by these projects, but also by the more explicit, and often graphically simplified, productions of post-modernist architects. Venturi and Scott Brown were joined by figures such as Michael Graves and Charles Moore in the US, Ricardo Bofill, Christian de Portzamparc, and James Stirling in Europe, and Arata Isozaki in Japan. Aldo Rossi, too, came to be seen as a key member of the movement. While some of the criticisms of modernism – including its lack of colour and diversity – were justified, the outcome was invariably kitsch, shorthand messages to the reviewers of these buildings. Venturi and Scott Brown's own Children's Museum in Houston, 1992, typically staked a claim for architecture as "fun" and "playful" while reducing the idea of classical architecture to a mere stage set – a prop – in front of an otherwise austere piece of architecture. The thinness of post-modern architecture as semiotic decoration was enabled and popularised by the relative affordability of its construction. For architects, post-modernism fulfilled the same role as pattern books in earlier times, allowing for the copying or reapplication of certain forms and motifs.

Charles Jencks' seminal publication *The Language of Post-Modern Architecture* (1977) announced the "death of modern architecture" and provided the movement with its own manifesto and theoretical framing. Soon after, a host of everyday and mundane buildings were dressed in post-modernist garb, all under the guise of providing the consumer with a more cheerful experience. One of the more ironic examples of post-modernism is its dressing up of modernist social housing schemes through their recladding – a visual erasure of their origin and an attempt to literally "kill" modern architecture.

Soon after the publication of *The Language of Post-Modern Architecture*, Jencks used his own 19th-century house in London's rarified Holland Park area as a laboratory for the exploration of meaning and symbolism in architecture. Working in collaboration with Terry Farrell, a former high-tech architect who had converted to post-modernism, Jencks transformed his house in a manner that seems to recall Sir John Soane's house, now a museum, as a precedent. The ornate and colourful interiors and furniture, many using painted MDF (medium density fibreboard) for their carcass, allowed for the easy construction of shapes and profiles such as the pediments, which were a prerequisite for most post-modern structures. The general accessibility of historic forms as an easily replicable and communicable "language" was a critical factor in the popularisation of the movement.

Jencks, well read, erudite and passionate about his ideas and causes, had planned to move out of his house and to turn it into a research centre and archive, but his untimely death in 2019 put the project on hold. He did, however, live long enough to witness his Thematic House – which he had intended to rename "Cosmic House", to reflect his more recent interests in landscape and cosmology – being given the seal of approval by Historic England in 2018. The house was awarded a Grade One listing, a category reserved for buildings of exceptional importance. Was this in recognition of the fact that the ideas it encapsulated had become part of history – a validation of the continuity of post-modernism – or was it perhaps a sign of renewed interest in what it has to offer us for the future?

The transition from modernism to post-modernism also coincided with an interest among scholars in the architecture of the Enlightenment – although perhaps it was no coincidence that Michael Graves was making drawings and buildings inspired by the likes of Claude Nicolas Ledoux at the same time that his colleague at Princeton, the historian Anthony Vidler, was busy writing about the French architect. Was it the historian who influenced the architect – or the architectural milieu that influenced the historian? Perhaps the seeds of the idea went back to Colin Rowe and his interest in the Viennese Jewish émigré historian Emil Kaufmann, whose writings on Ledoux date back to the 1930s. It is often hard to pinpoint the precise sources of influence. Still, the late 1970s and 1980s provided seemingly fertile opportunities for architecture to draw on history as an endless repository of forms.

Kaufmann credited Ledoux as the progenitor of the concept of "l'architecture parlante", denoting an architecture that speaks or reveals its function. Jencks' *The Language of Post-Modern Architecture* and the work of post-modern architects also helped to reaffirm the concept of architecture as language, as did post-structuralist discussions of architecture at the time. Post-modernist architecture, however, broke off the literal association between appearance and function pursued by 18th-century French visionary architects. In this way, Michael Graves was able to use the reference of

Ledoux's project for the House of the Inspector of Rivers – imagined with the river flowing through the building – as an ornament, an addition on the proposed façade of the unbuilt Fargo-Moorhead Cultural Center.

In 1988, some ten years after the publication of Jencks' book, a major exhibition on *Deconstructivist Architecture* was curated by Philip Johnson in association with Mark Wigley at the Museum of Modern Art in New York City. Johnson, poacher turned gamekeeper, was the founder in 1932 of the Department of Architecture and Design at MoMA. A former arch-modernist, he had also produced one of the most iconic buildings of the post-modern period, the AT&T building in Manhattan. Johnson declared that the show did not represent a movement, a style or a manifesto, but a body of work that revealed affiliations and similarities with Russian avant-garde art and constructivism. Most of the exhibited projects were unrealised competition schemes, and much of what he seemed to enjoy about them was encapsulated in his use of terms such as "pleasures of the unease" or "violated perfection", referring to the way they appeared to violate the right angles and cubes of modernism. But he had borrowed these terms, as he did most other things. He made no mention of "deconstruction", or what that had to do with the exhibition. That was left to others. Of the seven architects in the exhibition, Peter Eisenman was perhaps the only one who explicitly saw his work as a direct manifestation or expression of current philosophical theories, although others – Libeskind, Koolhaas and Tschumi – had all demonstrated an interest in surrealism and its potential influence on architecture.

What most of the architects shared, however, was their long connection with Alvin Boyarsky, chairman of the Architectural Association in London, who had mentored and supported them as students or teachers, or through exhibitions and publications at the school. In a way, the exhibition was a stealth celebration of Boyarsky's AA and of his influence – except for the fact that he was nowhere to be seen. He made only a cameo appearance towards the end of Johnson's seemingly endless list of acknowledgements, which filled two columns. No need for Johnson to worry about the complicated burden of influence. He was the one who had chosen the architects and discovered the formal similarities in their work.

Johnson turned out to be right. At least about the fact that deconstructivist architecture was not a movement. Invariably more connected with the academy than with practice, it did not have the staying power of post-modernism and was harder and more expensive to do well. Almost all the architects in the exhibition continue their practice, but their work is rarely framed in terms of deconstruction, or any other theory, for that matter. Architects generally seem to have developed a greater resistance to using theory as a formal and visual "language" of architecture or communicability.

Zaha Hadid was the only woman in the exhibition and the only architect to have not survived. Despite her tragic death, her practice remains active, with numerous large-scale projects across the globe. ZHA, as it has been rebranded, is also the only firm associated with the MoMA exhibition to pursue a specific theoretical methodology or style, namely parametric architecture or parametricism, a mode of design that is inseparable from contemporary computational and technological imaginaries and possibilities.

*In What Style Should We Build?* was the title of a pamphlet published in 1828 by a young German architect, Heinrich Hübsch. For Hübsch, technological advances in the 19th century had made the use of Greek neoclassical architecture obsolete. What was needed was a new architecture better suited to its time. The publication sparked a series of debates on the status of architecture and its relation to a temporally specific cultural condition, but it did not materialise in a new movement or style. Instead, the 19th century would be characterised by a plurality of styles.

Having been freed of the orthodoxies of modernism, are we now confronted with the same question that Hübsch asked almost two centuries ago? And if so, what are the ways in which architecture, and design more generally, might help to address our current societal predicaments, as well as our formal and spatial desires?

Architecture today, like its 19th-century predecessor, is once again an aesthetically subjective discipline – a profession based on the idea of taste, primarily linked to a subjective judgement that scrutinises the appearance of an artifice. In part, the challenge remains how to create the conditions for a greater sharing and articulation of value systems and aesthetic judgement through mutual conversation and dialogue. But part of the task necessitates a broader, deeper and more pluralistic understanding of history and what it can offer us. In his writings, Hübsch spoke about the importance and role of walls, ceilings, roofs, supports, windows and doors as the elements of style and how their forms changed according to the materials used.

Similar to Hübsch, the 2014 Venice Biennale of Architecture, *Elements of Architecture*, curated by Rem Koolhaas, put "under a microscope the fundamentals of buildings, used by any architect, anywhere, anytime: the floor, the wall, the ceiling, the roof, the door, the window …". "Anytime" meant historical, contemporary and future manifestations of these elements, which were proposed as "the fundamentals of building" and used in a manner slightly unexpected of someone with Koolhaas' attitude towards construction.

For an example of the mastery of the elements of building, we could look to the Church of St Peter in Klippan (1963–66), the last major commission of the Swedish architect Sigurd Lewerentz, whom Alison Smithson called one of the modern movement's "silent architects", a respresentative of its "non-polemic" and "nothing-to-do-with-packaging threads". Here, Lewerentz primarily used one material, brick, and worked closely with the construction foreman to ensure that only whole bricks were used throughout the building process. Walls, floors, ceilings and windows all attest to the haptic and sensorial capacities of architecture – rather than merely its visual qualities and means of communication.

Many architects today are considering the elements of architecture through a variety of materials and their formal and spatial capacities. In some instances, lightness is the most evident form of practice, while in others, it is the focus on solidity and mass that has inspired the architectural imagination. Whether light or heavy construction, it is the shift in emphasis from image to affect that best describes the transformation of architecture in the recent past. In addition to conventional dualisms such as opacity and transparency, other topics, including those of tonality, texture, reflection, colour and ornament, have assumed greater importance in the discussions of spatiality, as a key phenomenon that lies at the intersection of the physical and temporal conditions of a project. The shift from image to affect also represents a rebalancing between the visual and the experiential and, consequently, a more systematic engagement with the specific characteristics of a project's social, political and environmental conditions.

**39**

Architecture's exploration of its circumstantial conditions prioritises the given, but also recognises its productive possibilities. The plurality at the heart of the best versions of contemporary architecture is contingent on the way in which our imagination responds to a given or existing situation. The given also includes themes such as climate, environmental degradation, the availability of materials and other resources, all manner of inequities, lifestyle, habits and technologies of production. Each of these circumstances, whether tangible or intangible, provides a legitimate arena of architectural investigation.

Recent explorations of location, construction, sustainability and the use of the temporal and sensorial regimes of colour in architecture offer examples of how contemporary practice is reflecting on earlier influences and histories of the discipline to produce work that is at once investigative and a positive and dynamic experience for the user.

Like Pancho Guedes, a number of contemporary architects are also interested in the intersection of art and architecture. But for some, art is not just a way of being free as an architect; rather, it is about how the material explorations of architecture provide a dialogue that touches on topics as diverse as urbanisation and the social and political dimensions of practice, as well as questions of a more perceptual nature, such as flatness, vibrancy of colours and their illusionistic and associational capacities. These experiential and performative qualities of architecture also necessitate a responsiveness to the consideration of materials, resources, energy and modes of construction.

One of the more positive aspects of the post-1990s period, in architecture and design more broadly, is its role as a period of reflection. Reflections or rethinkings, however, can take many forms. Perhaps today we feel a nostalgia for the lack of intellectual tendencies and movements like Team X – not so much for the loss of a singular or identifiable architecture, but for the conversations, the camaraderie, the sharing of ideas and aspiring to a common purpose.

That is also why, at this point in time, the problematisation of influence might be a worthwhile endeavour, so long as we acknowledge the reciprocal and productive relations between influence and critique. The problematisation of influence might then be a means by which we can simultaneously construct temporal specificity and historic continuity with what has come before us.

Peter Cook

# Some Buildings and Entrails

**41**

The River Yare flows through Norwich and down to the easternmost point in England, through slightly dreamy, low-lying fields and close to a tiny Saxon church in which Louisa Hutton and Matthias Sauerbruch were married – several years after their first "date" at a party I had thrown in my Notting Hill Gate days. The atmosphere of these Norfolk lowlands suggests little visual rhetoric: more a question of nuance, and many invitations to quietly absorb the subtle changes of light, degrees of dampness or occasional fragments of constructed form that lie within the trees.

It was among those trees that Louisa had choreographed an array of tiny lights that, viewed from her family home across a wide lawn, became gently magical as the evening drew in. Complementary to this delicate setting was an undeniably metropolitan event: wonderful multistorey ice-cream towers, a high-powered rock group – both straight up from London, with Peter Smithson and Zaha Hadid among the many who would probably never forget the immaculacy of the event and its setting.

During the few years between my party and their wedding, the couple had coalesced around an architectural approach that not only inherited the necessary eye and sensibility suggested by Louisa's background, but also needed to incorporate some of the vigour I still remember in Matthias' drawings as he arrived in the AA Unit that Christine Hawley and I were teaching. His birthplace, Constance, was that agreeably "southern" city my German friends always refer to with a smile: a resort, but a "correct" one – it is almost in Switzerland. Certainly not misty and marshy Norfolk. Yet that energy and enthusiasm must have come from somewhere or something: was it a reaction to the blandness of the architectural discourse at the Hochschule der Künste in Berlin encountering the verve of the Architectural Association in the mid-1980s? Or had he perhaps inherited the mixture of energy and narrative quality that was present in the work of his father, the painter Hans Sauerbruch?

In combination – and maybe drawing upon such accumulated subtleties – Louisa and Matthias have been immensely visual, never shirking from giving something both form and colour. They have consistently maintained this throughout a period in which the architectural mainstream has been shy, or even dismissive, of both – and always with a fascinating combination of deftness and lyricism that successfully manipulates this combinatory approach. In doing so, they come close to challenging the starkness of their contemporaries.

Still, there are other layers that can be discussed as refinements: the four years Louisa spent in the office of Alison and Peter Smithson, and Matthias' six in the fledgling Office for Metropolitan Architecture (OMA). Backgrounds in which the rarefied atmosphere around the Smithsons would certainly have accentuated a consciousness of both purpose and discrimination and (maybe) a continuation of that English landscape – or where the excited atmosphere between the OMA founders, Elia Zenghelis and Rem Koolhaas, was to be enjoyed? It is a sign of the bond between Louisa and Matthias that the very contrast of these two experiences – periods long enough to be quite different from the name-hopping pattern of more recent graduates – enabled them to observe the strengths and weaknesses of the eyrie and the hothouse, to layer this upon their shared AA background – and possibly aim for something else.

It is a typical London story that their first expression as an office seems to have been their own house in Ledbury Road, in West London's Notting Hill. I seem to remember the usual architects' weeding out of a typical mid-Victorian row house with new insertions boldly coloured in a palette that is warmer than that of Luis Barragan, which can only have cheered them up in the London climate. From this starting point, one can, over the years, track their use of colour developing ever forward and responding to an increasing range of scales and locations.

Colour remains the feature most often mentioned by Berliners when the conversation turns to Sauerbruch and Hutton: for it would seem that even

**42**

after thirty years, this city, which has become their home and workplace, harbours a kernel of resistance to the charm of their buildings – and I use the term "charm" here in its most positive and non-cynical sense. Surely not a resistance to their abilities and professionalism? Surely not to their energetic and assiduous commitment towards energy conservation by determined application, sustained (in every sense) pursuit of method, and nifty devices. Surely not to their repeatedly demonstrated ability to operate the testy world of economic floor plates, gross-to-net ratios, consistent surfaces and "sensible" sections?

So perhaps Berlin has a problem with charm? Having had to assert itself among so many German state capitals and cultural ambiguity where West confronts East has perhaps led it to become heavy-footed, solid, digging its heels well into muddy fields ringed by waterlands. This may help to explain the way in which cities such as Munich and Hamburg have more readily taken them to their bosom? Certainly, there is a recurring characteristic among the buildings that have gone up in Berlin since Hans Scharoun's library – with colour rarely being mentioned, and an uneasiness with lyricism of line, waywardness of mass, any slithery skin or fine grain. Sauerbruch Hutton's refusal (in most cases) to make their buildings get in line, hug the street, succumb to the dogma of serried paths of primary structure dictating the envelope must come across as a tiresome deviation – and if it seems light, then surely it must be flimsy stuff.

But, of course, it isn't.

Winning the commission for, and building, the GSW Headquarters (1991–99) established the dialogue. Its descent onto the ground is already provocative: questioning an architectural culture obsessed with reaction against a recent memory of Scharoun and the Hansaviertel and positing a composition of parts that is already more reminiscent of a Cubist collage – or as Sauerbruch and Hutton describe it, "a field of mats" – ranging from that of a nut to a boomerang, but also skilfully accepting the existing four-square box into the mix. Surely this is not just a couple of kids playing with toys, for one of the boomerangs is engaged with subtly "pulling you into the main entrance", and the lines and positions of the parts respond to layers of reference that affect the site. Yet it remained their only substantial work in central Berlin for a long time, while they accelerated through a succession of competition wins that resulted in even more lyrical architecture – elsewhere.

Before itemising and comparing some of my favourites, I cannot resist the temptation to dwell upon this dilemma: why has dear, fascinating, racy, sinister, sophisticated old Berlin been such a "plodder" for much of the last forty years? Why has the Hauptbahnhof, having inherited the machine-drama of two main lines crossing each other in space, had to grip it in unbelievably chunky metal sticks? Why is Frank Gehry's ebullience trapped *inside* a pompous stone box? What happened to the ghosts of Poelzig, Mendelsohn and Scharoun? Why is everything so *HEAVY*? Encouraged and stultified by the reactionary Hans Stimmann – who as the Berlin Senate's director of building from 1991 to 1996 and again from 1999 to 2006 kept the city in his iron grasp – the ponderous aspect of Prussian thinking held sway just as Berlin was returning to a state of completeness.

Two amoeba-like objects appear in an industrial complex on the edge of Adlershof, where they create moments of delight as they flirt with each other. The polychromy used on the structure to transcend the simple tectonics of

**43**

its prefab construction, together with colour on the solar louvres, is a combination we shall see iterated, developed and endlessly toyed with – sometimes more boldly, sometimes more subtly. Two developing strands: that of the pursuit of low-energy building along with the continuing evolution of the undulating edge. The delight of the sinuous line is added to the inevitable joy in using colour – but then becomes really challenged in the large complex of the Federal Environmental Agency in Dessau, conceived in 1998.

The "double snake" of a plan has to master a wide variety of elements, some of which break out of the "ribbony" carcass into fractured steel and glass. It is a heroic achievement – way beyond the brief and any reasonable expectancy – questioning the dogmatics, if you like, of the hallowed Bauhaus buildings in that same city. And yet, and yet, one feels that in their work, too, there was at that moment an itch to look forward to a more *total* piece of architecture. Undoubtedly, the ADAC Headquarters in Munich represents another step: as at GSW, the proposition of tower-on-podium – which we all grew up with, lectured on the significance of Skidmore, Owings & Merrill's 1950s Lever House in New York – is pushed to a poetic degree that disciples of the American Mies or SOM would not have contemplated – nor have wished. The tower itself undulates and then, my God, sits out from a podium that lyrically lurches (excuse the term) into a starfish figuration. Moreover, it is wasp-coloured – at least in the general sense, as you see other pastel tones when you peer at the detail of the skin.

There is a confidence – and perhaps a growing resistance - to making too many sensitive but fiddly responses at once, which is a characteristic of British architecture in particular. At this point, it is, of course, impossible for me to claim impartiality, for their Ministry for Urban Development and the Environment in Hamburg (2009–13) is fairly simultaneous to the Law Faculty that Gavin Robotham and I built in Vienna: there are U-shaped undulations in a ribbon, there are gradated horizontals of bright colour, there are pieces of the building curving and swinging out. It is an alliance of instincts perhaps, and not a dead ringer. Yet there is probably a shared nerve ending that was never totally overridden by the mainline modernist training – which spanned both generations – and linked the Bauhaus and SOM and all of that to the Rational tradition. Reyner Banham wrote about this and was one of the first to draw our attention to Poelzig, to legitimise Häring and to include Finsterlin in the direct line of discussable architecture. When Sauerbruch and Hutton (or we) swing outwards, we swing with Hans Luckhardt's concert hall project of 1920, or Bernhard Hoetger's naughty goings-on in Bremen ("Don't look at him," I hear the hardliners screech, "he wasn't even an architect"). But mention Hugo Häring's Gut Garkau farm near Lübeck and they get twitchy, and even more nervous about Scharoun's Schminke House in Löbau, which chooses just when to swing out into overlapping voluptuousness that actually emerges from the clear and circumspect modernism of the main body of the building. Not to mention Erich Mendelsohn's Einstein Tower in Potsdam. There was a funny correlation of information that I used to get before I finally got to see it myself in the 1990s. A certain type of reporter would say, "It's actually very small" or "It's not in good condition" or some such. As with the response to GSW, it was a code for saying, "We shouldn't do such things."

The Hamburg building marries this same nerve ending with an even further attack upon the sanctity of the podium: each swing of the snake gallantly riding out over the baseline – at last, the over-building need not be inhibited by the under-building. The colouration, too, begins to break ranks and performs its own more staccato counterpoint. By the time of the Municpal Savings

44

Bank in Oberhausen (2004–07) or the Oval Offices in Cologne (2010), the language had already become fluent, with an especially pertinent development, whereby the staircases take on that special gliding-twisting magic remembered in my mind from those grainy photographs of the descending theatre staircases in the Grosses Schauspielhaus designed by Hans Poelzig in 1919. Making magic out of such a condition is surely the most delightful moment in Scharoun's Philharmonie. Once again, one has the feeling that our heroes are the entwined inheritors of the wayward, gently drifting English sense of narrative – or paths that gently ride in the interpretation of the Smithsons added to this generally supressed wing of German invention – too viciously dismissed as "expressionism". The central stair at Oberhausen thus flies free of its obligations and uses a greenish-yellow for the outer rim that is *just* enough to capture the bright light of the inner one.

Great stuff.

Light wells, seductive nods of the forms of the red building towards the green building, and the three-dimensional snaking of staircases combine in a language that is, so to say, really "swinging". Of course, my enthusiasm gathers pace, in particular, towards buildings that set up a figure within an un-insistent field. A month ago, I let that photograph of the Cologne buildings peering out of the mist rest for almost a minute, to conclude a Zoomed lecture that had started with the shadow of a grim block of a recent Belgian building also peering out of the mist. My point concerned the issue of delight, which is almost always there in the work under discussion. So, it is reasonable, like all grim academics, to thrust the proposition further. I take a look at the Saint-Georges Centre in Geneva of 2012 and then at 2 New Ludgate in London. Both have a similar language around pinkish skins and subtly deviant colour, undulating near – but never dogmatically along – roughly 100-year-old commercial streets. Yet they are both forced to fit into the closer urban grain: in Geneva, offering a surprise near-enclosure of outside space at the rear – as if to tempt this Calvinist city to enjoy such patches of space. Even more tightly constrained in London, opportunities are somehow found to shift mood through colour away from the street – perhaps enjoying the sneaky old tradition of passageways that remains.

In this respect, the more recent M9 Museum in Mestre is very aware of its obligations towards what we might loosely call the Camillo Sitte school of urban observation. Of its sensitivity there is no doubt, but for my taste, the ordinance of sharp lines leads to a certain dogmatism, in ways not intended. It certainly is not Italian dusty concrete or stucco, but is, for me, too compromised. Having reached such voluptuous joy in the north, it is as if the weight of Italy's insistence upon *culture and grain* makes them a little nervous. Not that they eschew sorties into the angular elsewhere. In the Experimenta project for Heilbronn, a different language was designed in 2013: a jagged series of rotating wraps creates a ribbon of exposed glass that is contrasted with solid swathes. Now completed and almost entirely of glass, the building looks its best at night, when the colour of the interior shines forth.

Ongoing at the same time is surely one of their cleverest exercises. Allowed to return to the centre of Berlin in 2014, near the foot of the TV Tower, their Alea 101 building at Alexanderplatz added a deliberate slice of white building, sandwiching – in a somewhat skewed way – a black glass filling that sits on a very slightly wayward, clear glass base. So far so good, but the building then reveals their characteristic lyricism as it explodes from within with a beautiful courtyard and the gliding roof buildings.

**45**

They have made so many good buildings that, once again, I am drawn detective-like towards some of the eccentric one-offs before moving on to a couple more classics. There is the "wrap-over" Experimental Factory in Magdeburg (1998–2001), a format that has attracted Bernard Tschumi (2015), Diller Scofidio + Renfro (2003–06) and Neil Denari (2014), to name but three sets of architects for whom I have great regard. In the end, of course, it is the flanking figuration that remains in the mind's eye, and the melting of wall into roof into wall into roof remains a curiously limited pursuit that appeals to each of these architects, who are, after all, no mean intellects. I am similarly drawn to the retro-fit Munich Re (2009–11), where the architects were obliged to merely re-skin an existing four-square structure. Intriguingly, and pleasingly, it somehow "sags" the plan between the verticals. This may seem a soft option, but then, to its credit, it is *just* that – choosing neither to lose the generative items nor to let them dictate rectangularity. It is a virtuoso cadenza lilting into and out of the predesignated theme – with a developed Sauerbruch Hutton skin and colour, of course.

And so to the K House in friendly Munich. Funny that, because to those of us from the northern swamps, Munich seems very pleased with itself, yet Louisa and Matthias have made most of their best things there. The K House (and I wonder who this lucky "K" can be) is at once compact and quite four-square in the interior, while lazily, lyrically meandering on the outside. Perhaps more successfully than in Mestre, creating a fine grain of colour and then blistering out, Garkau-like from the flow, just once or twice.

If creating a private house is a classic challenge, then making an unfettered display statement is even more so. Their colour installation at the 2014 group exhibition *How Soon Is Now* was a response to the seminal London exhibition *This Is Tomorrow*, held at London's Whitechapel Art Gallery in 1956. I, personally, was detached from that London show by a generation, although both Louisa and I have a connection to it through Peter Smithson (as his student and his assistant, respectively). For their 2014 installation, Louisa and Matthias chose to invoke the figure of Richard Hamilton as reference. A tricky call, since he was not only a painter of great skill and scholar of technique, but also a man of intense political commitment, which found its way through reference to haunting imagery – such as the dated tape recorder in *Just what is it that makes today's homes so different?* (1956) or his painting a decade or so later of Mick Jagger and art dealer Robert Fraser handcuffed together in a police van. Sauerbruch Hutton choose to remain abstract, making colour their statement (or so it seems) – which is delightful.

For it is that elusive sense of "eye" that Matthias and Louisa both have. It is surely linked to the same discriminatory talent that seems to know just how much overt demonstration of serious energy considerations can be incorporated into an aesthetic mode or expressive "run". Most of all, though, it shines through in the Brandhorst Museum (2005–09) in Munich, where a deceptively simple division of upper and lower levels is articulated by a substantial band of horizontal glazing (which deals with the projection of natural light into the lower galleries). The upper galleries have a skilfully developed top light / laylight system, again, to deal with natural light. The colour of the façade is then apportioned: thin ceramic battens onto a metal skin, with a paler mix for the upper part and stronger hues for the lower. It works. It fits the serenity of Munich, forming an "open T" with the pre-existing building and yet completely original to itself. The latter with enviable deftness.

In my mind's eye, I can see a certain Sauerbruch Hutton building that might find its way into a piece of space somewhere, in which this surface of thin, vertical ceramic (or metal or timber) strips acts as the medium of one of their sexy, tantalising pavilions. I hear that they are involved in prefabrication for housing. Good, good. They've got plenty of oomph going and a large, trusted and no doubt talented team slowly taking over. Good, good.

Please realise for me this dream of wayward snakes and slats of gradual kaleidoscopic surprise. I can almost see it.

47

**48**

Barry Bergdoll

# Sustaining the City

Just a year after citizens of the German Democratic Republic surged through the Berlin Wall in November 1989 in pale, pastel-toned Trabants (the standard-issue car of the GDR), two young architects in London, Louisa Hutton and Matthias Sauerbruch, staged a robustly colourful architectural vision of a newly reunited city. The GSW tower, selected in a design competition in 1990 and opened in 1999, broke above the uniform cornice lines of the Friedrichstraße area and entered into a dialogue with a bland modernist tower of 1961, to which it was, in fact, technically but an addition. With a curved, glazed curtain wall set before a system of sun-shading panels in reds, pinks and oranges that were in turn all set against the often grey skies over Berlin, just a few hundred metres from Checkpoint Charlie, Sauerbruch

Hutton's GSW heralded new thinking not only about Berlin, but about cities in general. A jaunty cantilevered oval "pillbox" element – anchoring the old and new towers like a peg – was wrapped in metallic bands of greens and yellows alternating with fenestration. Here was a possible palette for the closing moments of Berlin's traumatic 20th century at a spot on the periphery of West Berlin that was suddenly at the very centre of the new capital of reunified Germany. The colourfulness was anything but decorative; it was a statement about architecture itself, with echoes of the ways in which polychromy has punctuated the history of rethinking architecture's social significance and potential, especially in the emerging metropolis – from the romantic critique of neoclassicism in the 1830s, to the colouristic reaction to the uniformity of Haussmannian Paris in the 1880s, to incipient German expressionism with Paul Scheerbart's line of poetry "Coloured glass destroys hatred" on Bruno Taut's Glass House at the 1914 Werkbund exhibition.

By 1999, an orderly procession of new buildings up and down Friedrichstraße had taken their cues from prescriptions by Berlin's *Senatsbaudirektor* to recapture the supposedly harmonious state of the city's urban morphology as it was prior to the bombings of the Second World War and the subsequent destructions of post-war development. Berlin was seen as the great stage for the "critical reconstruction" of the European city, first essayed in the IBA of 1987, and given new impetus by reunification and the return of much of the Federal Republic's government functions from Bonn to Berlin. Sauerbruch and Hutton did not disagree with the ethos of a new urbanity, but their approach and the range of issues they embraced set their work apart and launched a career of research into reinvigorating urban environments, particularly former peripheries, with a more complex toolbox of strategies that nearly always included their colourful material palette. Upon moving their office from London to Berlin in the early 1990s to supervise construction of their surprise victory in the GSW competition, they announced a complex new urban attitude – one that accepted the complexities of Berlin's layers of construction and destruction, of continuity and change – in a building that expressed optimism for a new millennium in every aspect: from pioneering research into sustainable energy solutions to a composition that changed with the perspective of the viewer, whether on foot or in a vehicle, at this newly busy intersection.

I still remember the moment in 1999, driving along Kochstraße (today Rudi-Dutschke-Straße), when a colourful greenish oval form cantilevered in mid-air suddenly appeared at the edge of the windscreen of my rental car like a UFO in a tracking shot. It was quickly followed by the red and orange fenestration of a glazed, boomerang-shaped office tower, two curvilinear forms in this rectilinear city. The components of this urban puzzle – it became clear once I stopped to understand – anchored a composition clustered around and locked in with a mundane 1960s office tower, which I had somehow never noticed in previous years during countless walks in this neighbourhood, which lay in the shadow of the Cold War's fault line. In the twenty years I had been coming to Berlin for research, I had negotiated these liminal streets many times, first in the early 1980s in an effort to understand Karl Friedrich Schinkel's Berlin of the 1820s and 1830s even as his projects were now separated by a heavily armed international boundary. Almost two decades later, I was now seeking to comprehend – for a planned MoMA exhibition (*Mies in Berlin*, 2001) – the urban context for all the projects that had been either built or projected by Mies van der Rohe during the three decades he was in quest of a new idiom and expression for a metropolitan architecture honed in the vibrant cross-currents of Weimar Berlin. With the appearance of the

**49**

pillbox and the boomerang, and the freedom of their polychromy, I felt as though either I had accidentally channel-surfed to another temporal and urban frequency, or here was evidence of a new project for building in a city on the brink of a new century, in which both the political and the environmental ravishes of the 20th century were to be confronted head-on, all the while seeking an architecture with the promise of a new civic realm, one that might even invite joy and pleasure as essential elements of construction. The publicly accessible lobby connecting two streets was only the beginning, while above, the offices set new standards for energy efficiency.

It would be another few years before I met Louisa Hutton and Matthias Sauerbruch and began to follow their work not only on a meandering *Stadtbummel* – since by now, I had encountered the Fire and Police Station in the reanimated Spreebogen district from the elevated S-Bahn on its way to Friedrichstraße, as well as on foot – but equally by watching projects unfold in their Berlin office. One thing was clear: in the spirit of Schinkel and Mies, architects formed by Berlin, who also set out to form Berlin by the insertion of buildings that changed the urban setting through connections and dialogues, even if confined to their respective building sites, Sauerbruch Hutton proposed a new urbanity for architecture.

Just after the opening of the Brandhorst Museum, which more or less completed the museum quarter in Munich's Schwabing district, I was invited to contribute an essay on Sauerbruch Hutton's work for a monographic issue of the Spanish periodical *2G* (No. 52, 2009). As a historian of 19th-century architecture by training, and then a curator of architecture at New York's Museum of Modern Art (where I was proud to add drawings and a model of the GSW project to the permanent collection), I took this essay as an occasion to consider two decades of the architects' work synthetically at the very moment in which they completed their first museum, a project notable in its relationship to one of the most important museum buildings of the 19th century: Leo von Klenze's Alte Pinakotek, the first element of what was already emerging as a cultural forum in the mid-19th century. That essay led me to experience first-hand the urban attitude not only of this new Munich building, but of their recent structures in Frankfurt, Cologne and Dessau, and also in Sheffield in the UK. Recurrent preoccupations and strategies emerged from this intense tour: the exquisite attention to rhythms and patterns in everything, from the way light filters into newly created interior public space to the careful compositions of façades that always enter into dialogue with the ways people use and live in cities, particularly cities that have been wounded and repaired on numerous occasions; the seamless introduction of environmental and sustainable strategies as part of the very fabric of the buildings; and a non-imitative animation of the dialogue between the as-found and possible future city. Existing traces found on the sites they take on provide cues to the formulation of the various project *partis*, their urban scenographies and even their colour palettes. The studio then creates new constellations that in turn respond to the existing, even as they often conjure up surprising urban qualities where others could scarcely have imagined the potential.

Dessau is a superb example of this. Here, for the first time, the characteristic sinuosity of a building's integration with city and landscape enhances the experience of users, from those who spend their days in the offices of the federal agency, to visitors who traverse the garden atrium embraced by the sinewy branches of the office space, to all kinds of passers-by – even those who experience the colourful façade patterns at different speeds from cars on the nearby roadway or from local and express DB trains on the major north-south rail line that borders the site to the west. One understands the coloured sketches characteristic of the practice's analysis of a situation almost as film storyboards, thinking of projects in relationship to the complex overlay of different speeds of perception in the city.

Now that Sauerbruch Hutton have completed another decade of practice since that summary in *2G*, adding an ever more diverse portfolio of architectural types with an ever more prominent role for public and cultural projects, along with their finesse in private sector projects, the steadfast civic ethos and commitment has become even clearer. If the formal elements develop from an existing and coherent aesthetic and approach, the integration of sustainable innovations remains in the vanguard. Key themes have been hallmarks of projects from the earliest sketches reproduced in the practice's now two-volume *archive* compendium. These include: responding to an urban situation with its diverse users and speeds of encounter; adding new elements to an existing landscape to enhance both what is found and what can be created; and focusing on a vocabulary of architecture that – as I observed in 2009 – is "as much about the end users of buildings as about its authors" (p. 4) through the creation of a "dialogue (…) in which the architect no longer, as so often in the 1970s, relinquishes the role of providing strong signature form". In 2021, as the world seeks to emerge from a year of on-and-off confinement, the desire to interact in public space has never been more pent up. Two cultural buildings recently completed by Sauerbruch Hutton are already starting to help in the recovery of the civic and public sphere, that is to say, in our communal life, which, in this year of withdrawal and turmoil, has been in such unwilling retreat.

Both M9 in Mestre and Experimenta in Heilbronn are public projects that reimagine not only largely disused historic structures – a 16th-century former convent in the case of Mestre, an early 20th-century warehouse in Heilbronn – but do so in order to create veritable cities in miniature, reanimating districts, connections and places that transform local public life. This is a long way from the notion of the museum as a treasure box or temple, set atop a podium and lifted above the city, as was the case in the 19th-century buildings of Berlin's museum complex, even if Schinkel had launched the new building type in north Germany with the image of the colonnaded stoa, the most publicly accessible structure of the ancient Athenian Agora. Even if the idea of a new agora had been a guiding concept between Berlin's Kulturforum of museum buildings next to Mies van der Rohe's archetypical modernist art temple, the Neue Nationalgalerie, the result was essentially stillborn. Matthias Sauerbruch's cogent critique of the Kulturforum, delivered at a 2013 symposium in conjunction with the exhibition *Culture: City* at Berlin's Akademie der Künste (and reprinted in *sauerbruch hutton. archive 2* in 2016), is not only an insightful text of historical and morphological analysis, but a veritable programme for the two museums in the Veneto and in Württemberg, which mark the latest stage in the practice's commitment to reanimating urban life even in a period in which digital tools have fundamentally changed both private and public life. "Instead of the pulsating heart of the city," at the Kulturforum, Sauerbruch notes, "one encounters a monoculture of high-calibre cultural events in more or less isolated buildings that make little or no contribution to public space" (p. 238). If the appeal was aimed, albeit unsuccessfully, at winning a role in the much-needed revisions of this project during the final days of West Germany and Berlin (West), the analysis remains one that served as the basis for the thinking and designing that bore fruit some years later not only in the public buildings for Mestre and

**51**

Heilbronn, but in an impressive array of other projects at various urban scales. Just as digital devices have continually eroded boundaries between commerce and culture, between home and office – exacerbated by the transition to remote work prompted by the Covid-19 pandemic of 2020–21 – so the work of Sauerbruch Hutton has embraced the fluidity of functions and the mixture of uses and users that together contribute to urban vibrancy and the creation of particular qualities of places.

M9 is a project that functions as meaningfully for the citizens of Mestre who pass by and through the complex on a daily basis as it does for visitors from afar who come to explore the exhibitions and various events programmed by the cultural institution. The hope is that they might even be tempted to stop in Mestre before heading over to Venice, and not only because the food is often better. The museum hosts an interactive exhibition of 20th-century history and culture, as well as changing displays in an exquisitely scaled top-lit gallery in the building's upper reaches. But even those who don't venture in will gravitate to a site that holds not only new buildings of great urban presence, but also a new public square, a gathering place, as well as a diagonal shortcut that has already changed pedestrian patterns in Mestre. Paths through the city have been created that interweave both the renovated convent – its great, lightly roofed, arcaded cloister now a place of public assembly – and the new buildings with the surrounding urban fabric. The journey up towards the sky-lit gallery on the uppermost floor – which beckons as a culmination of the journey – is one of the most exciting yet conceived by the practice. Most striking is not only the scale of the grand stair and the rhythm of ascent it creates against a continually changing experience provided by the colour schemes of the façades, but also the shifting views it offers of this new collection of buildings, which form an integral part of the city.

In *nuce*, this approach to urban fabric, a dialogue of complex geometries in which new sculptural elements play against the carving of space in an urban block, was, in fact, an essential part of the architects' approach to the GSW project some thirty years ago. But here, the creation of space in the city lives up to the idea of the urban scene as proposed by Sebastiano Serlio – namely the staging of buildings as the creation of urban mood – and to the analyses of the dialogue between solids and voids, both constructed, as formulated in Austrian urbanist Camillo Sitte's influential *The Art of Building Cities: City Building According to Its Artistic Fundamentals*, published in 1889, precisely a century before German reunification. For a museum that traces 20th-century history and culture even as it reanimates architectural fragments from the Renaissance, this dialogue of past and emerging present could not be more apt.

Even more than in Mestre, the Science Centre in Heilbronn echoes its curatorial vision in an architecture that functions on the local as well as regional and national levels. The scientific director requested a place of interactive learning in which experience and experiment lead to knowledge rather than the static, didactic communication of preconceived ideas. Sauerbruch Hutton responded with a building whose helical form and path – a theme that runs through some of the most daringly experimental museum buildings of the 20th century, from Frank Lloyd Wright's Guggenheim Museum in New York (1959) to Alvaro Siza's Iberê Camargo Museum in Porto Alegre, Brazil (2008) – plays a most sophisticated dialogue between inward-focused learning areas and the wider environment in which it stands. The shifting forms of the spiral circulation path provide a journey that takes in an orchestrated sequence of panoramas of the city of Heilbronn and the surrounding

**52**

Neckar region, views of urban grit and scenic agriculture worthy of another 19th-century ideal, Patrick Geddes' idea of the Index Museum – first essayed in his famous Outlook Tower, which opened in Edinburgh's Old Town in 1892 – where display and a new perception of the everyday were integral parts of his vision for a museum imbued with the idea of regenerating the city.

As always in a research-oriented architectural practice, these projects are not end points but rather way stations on a journey that began with the unexpected chance to propose a vision of urbanity for a reunited Berlin. Some of Sauerbruch and Hutton's most potent recent investigations into urban renewal take the form of intense material research into new possibilities for timber construction at every scale, from an exquisite small church in Cologne – the Immanuel Church and Parish Centre (2009–13) – to the Universal Design Quarter in Hamburg (2016–17), the world's largest residential building in modular timber construction at the time of its completion. Every month brings new stories of architects experimenting with the latest timber products, and almost continuously updated statistics on the environmental benefits and financial savings of greater reliance on renewable resources such as timber, starting, of course, with a reduction in the release of sequestered carbon into the environment. Sauerbruch and Hutton are not latecomers to the game. Their ever more focused attention on this material over the last twenty-five years has built on themes and values that have been at the heart of their endeavours from the very earliest projects. The Environmental Agency in Dessau (completed in 2005) displays its engagement into renewable building materials, appropriately enough, with its sinuous façades of all-timber panels. Recognised as a prototypical model for sustainable design and construction in Germany, it was awarded the DGNB's first gold certificate, the highest accolade when the DGNB (German Sustainable Building Council) was founded in 2007. Sauerbruch's insightful text "What Does Sustainability Look Like?", published in *sauerbruch hutton. archive 1* (2006), is, in this sense, a manifesto for the incorporation of the practice's research into a spatial and material aesthetics of timber within their long-standing commitment towards the production of responsible – and desirable – architecture and urbanism. Of all European metropolises, perhaps none is more defined by woodland than Berlin. Despite this essentially mineral city's reputation of hyperdensity – established by the publication in 1930 of Werner Hegemann's *Das steinerne Berlin* – the German capital went on to establish for itself one of the best balances between built and wooded space of any European city since it passed the Greater Berlin Act of 1920. In this sense, Berlin could be a laboratory for thinking of wood holistically, from the maintenance of forests to the production of buildings.

53

Over the last fifteen years, Sauerbruch and Hutton have progressively expanded their practice into low-impact energy design solutions that include the recycling and upgrading of inherited buildings on already occupied sites, and recognise the potential of individual interventions into existing urban morphologies to change larger patterns and possibilities of daily urban habitat. As always, the technical aspects of their investigations are integrated within the broader aims of their various architectural projects. An exquisitely honed sensibility for the capacity of structure and pattern to give rhythm to both interior and urban spaces created by new buildings has always been a hallmark of their work. And this sensibility is mastered across scales, from small buildings to entire urban complexes. This has been equally the case in the last decade of research into a greater role for timber construction, from the judicious application of the timber on the interior and exterior of the Immanuel Church in Cologne to their modular student residence created as part of the Universal Design Quarter in Hamburg. To work in timber is inevitably to relate to the larger cycles of nature and the human cycles of production. Nothing could illustrate this more clearly than the Cologne church set in a mature stand of trees of different species. The church attains its spatial rhythms and surface effects in equal measure through the exploration of different ways of deploying wood, from engineered timber columns and beams to the development of an exterior cladding of diagonal planks in alternating orientations, and by paying acute attention to the hues and textures of the unclad timber panels themselves. Here, thirty years of research into colour is literally merged with the nature of materials, quietly contemplative for this sacred space animated by a study of the effects of natural light – just as the marriage of ceramic and colour in the exterior of the Brandhorst Museum in Munich makes the structure an active component in the vibrancy of the urban neighbourhood of museums and shops.

The embrace of timber in key recent projects of the practice is free of any nostalgia, just as their work has reconstructed urbanity without recourse to pastiche from Sauerbruch and Hutton's first appearance on the Berlin scene some three decades ago. In Hamburg, reinforced concrete and modular timber construction achieve a symbiotic relationship between the selective and strategic use of concrete to create a ground-floor "table" with the rapid delivery of craned-in modular units that bring all the richness of the bespoke Cologne church design to the efficiencies of prefabrication in both the manufacture of building elements and the operations of the construction site.

Perhaps nothing could mark the thirtieth anniversary of the GSW building more poetically than one of their most recently completed projects: the addition to the Berlin Metropolitan School (2014–20) in Berlin-Mitte. Just as the clients of GSW refused to consider a banal building of West Berlin's early years of economic growth as a throwaway in the emerging glamour of the reunified Berlin of the early 1990s, so the opportunity to add to one of the last prefab school buildings of the German Democratic Republic to be completed – in 1987, less than three years before the dramatic events of 1989–90 led to German reunification – came as a welcome assignment. Sauerbruch and Hutton transformed the building complex through the addition of two floors for classrooms, as well as dramatic double-height spaces for performance, a music room, dance room and library, as well as an urban roof garden – all this while classes continued inside this building complex, which has served the private Berlin Metropolitan School since 2004. They exploited the advantages of prefabricated timber construction as a lightweight, self-finished material that can easily be mass-customized. This modest project is sustainable not only in its material manifestation, but in social and historic terms as well. Research into the efficiencies of industrial construction methods had been one of the hallmarks of the GDR's building culture. In a period when a reunited Germany has too often proceeded to disassemble the cultural and material legacy of its former eastern half – nowhere more famously than the demolition a short distance away of the Palast der Republik in order to create a pastiche of the former Hohenzollern Stadtschloss – Sauerbruch and Hutton have layered the fruits of recent developments in prefabrication – now addressing the overall ecological agenda – onto one of the last projects that demonstrated the GDR's own commitment to system building. The resulting palimpsest is not only a reconciliation with the realities of Germany's 20th-century history, it is an embrace of the attitude necessary for our occupation of the planet in the 21st.

Kristin Feireiss

# Free Thought, Free Form

**55**

On 16 January 1992, two doyens of 20th-century international architectural history met for the first time: the seminal architect Philip Johnson, the New York architecture scene's most influential power broker, and Julius Posener, the legendary Berlin architectural historian, university lecturer and philanthropist. They were bending over a model of the winning design for an extension to the GSW high-rise in Berlin by the German-British architect couple Sauerbruch Hutton. Both Johnson and Posener were convinced that this project, one of the first high-rises worldwide designed according to ecological principles, would send out a signal that post-reunification Berlin was moving into a new era. That moment, which also marked a turning point in the history of the skyscraper, is captured in a black-and-white photograph taken when the Sauerbruch Hutton exhibition opened in our Aedes

Architekturforum at Savignyplatz in Berlin. The ensuing response from the media and the public helped to take the wind out of the sails of critics in district and municipal administrations, who had felt that the design was at odds with their conservative architectural policy.

The extension to the GSW Headquarters in Berlin-Kreuzberg, near Checkpoint Charlie, staunchly defended throughout by managing directors Hans-Jörg Duvigneau and Gero Luckow, was officially opened on 2 September 1999. This structure played a pioneering role in the implementation of the most stringent sustainability requirements for high-rise – and other – buildings. Its striking colourful façade conceals an ingenious energy-saving concept and an unusual natural ventilation system: the louvre blinds move in response to shifting light levels throughout the day, and to changes in the weather, thus both protecting the building's interior and altering its external appearance. It is an early example of Sauerbruch Hutton's conviction that there is no contradiction between the mandates of sustainability and the need to address sensory perception. In the wake of the GSW high-rise, the architects continued to set the bar high in all of their subsequent projects, keeping apace of topical, rapidly developing expertise in the field of sustainability, while also forging ahead on the basis of their own research.

A flashback: the history I share with Matthias Sauerbruch and Louisa Hutton began in 1980 when Aedes Architekturforum opened in Grolmanstraße with an exhibition about London-based architects Alison and Peter Smithson; that was where we first met and laid the foundations for a lasting friendship. Our first joint project was with Matthias – Sauerbruch Hutton's Berlin office was not established until 1993, four years after their joint office had first opened in London – when he participated in the central exhibition for "Berlin – European Capital of Culture 1989", which I had been commissioned to curate by the Berlin Senate. Encompassing eighty-two architects from sixteen countries, the name of the exhibition was *Berlin: Monument or Model? – Architectural Projects for the Turn of the 21st Century*.

The theme of the urban landscape had already filtered through into Matthias Sauerbruch's visionary design even back then, in the late 1980s, in large-format charcoal drawings that depicted the industrial port facilities at Westhafen in north-west Berlin bisected by a huge glass strip. Elaborating on Scharoun's vision of an urban landscape literally as "built mountains", Sauerbruch Hutton deployed the concept in a more metaphorical spirit, both here and subsequently. They view the cityscape as an aleatoric composition that springs from an agglomeration of various urban backdrops and the layering of heterogeneous traces of history. When Matthias Sauerbruch wrote in the text accompanying his contribution to the exhibition: "The 'reconstructed city' provides a drama that stages horror vacui and wishful thinking as urban theatre," it was tantamount to declaring war on Berlin's architectural policy of that era, which in the 1990s, and even in the early 21st century, went all out to promote "critical reconstruction" of the historical city. Against this background, it comes as no surprise that new projects or invitations to participate in non-open competitions were few and far between for them in Berlin over the next twenty years, although the global success of the GSW high-rise catapulted the young practice overnight into the ranks of top architects. The only exceptions to that general trend were the Photonics Centre in Berlin-Adlershof and the combined Fire and Police Station in Berlin's government district.

Over the decades, the relationship with Louisa Hutton and Matthias Sauerbruch, in conjunction with the professional paths pursued by my partner Hans-Jürgen Commerell and myself – linking their practice of architecture and our role as architectural commentators – have given rise to a number of joint projects, such as a further Aedes exhibition of their work in 2000, with the somewhat cryptic title *WYSIWYG*. Their exhibition installation, designed specifically for the gallery, which was tucked into the arches beneath the train tracks, encompassed a particularly remarkable aspect: they presented not only their architectural projects, but also the practice's spatial use of colour, which led to an intriguing interplay between two- and three-dimensionality. Polychromy was not only a central theme in this exhibition, it also constitutes a significant feature in Sauerbruch Hutton's overall oeuvre.

Pondering how to describe the significance of their philosophy in just a few insightful words, I turn to architectural historian Jürgen Tietz and his publication *What is good architecture ?* Tietz had asked me, along with twenty other international authors, to cite just one building in our replies – which once again led me to Sauerbruch Hutton. I immediately selected the Federal Environmental Agency in Dessau, which had just opened in 2005. Even today, looking back more than fifteen years later, my choice at the time remains as valid as ever. If I had to put it in a nutshell, I would say that it is the atmosphere of this place that has stayed with me. What is astonishing is that this is a building used mainly for administration, not as a cultural institution – such as a museum, a library or an opera house – where it is always so much easier to develop and showcase architectonic qualities.

In my response to Tietz's question, I described the intuitive sense of well-being that embraces you in the generous atrium, thanks mostly to its proportions, materiality, colour and play of light. This visceral perception is then complemented by an awareness of particular aspects of urban planning, as well as by various architectural and ecological aspects of the design. The building adapts to the site's industrial topography while simultaneously nurturing a park of natural textures both inside and out. In this way, the project revitalises a heterogeneous urban space at the interface of city and landscape.

I then attempted to put together a list of criteria that determine what makes good architecture and settled upon the following five points: a holistic inter-disciplinary approach; an awareness of a place's historical identity; dealing responsibly with ecological concerns; a unity of form and content, of architecture and use; ferreting out, unifying and implementing not just the client's needs and wishes, but also those of users. Bringing all these strands together conceptually and combining them into a unified design is the hallmark of good architecture for me: architecture grows from within rather than simply being applied as a façade.

Rereading my text, I realise that the criteria I described back then, with the Federal Environmental Agency in mind, continue to apply to this day to all of Sauerbruch Hutton's other buildings – including those in the realm of culture – such as the Brandhorst Museum, inaugurated in Munich in 2009, Experimenta in Heilbronn, completed ten years later, or the M9 Museum District, recently opened to the public in Venice-Mestre.

In my view, the aspects that make Sauerbruch Hutton's architecture so special are its joyful presence, visible from afar, and appealing gestures that stimulate the urban surroundings while also being manifested in the building per se: a spatial interplay of delimiting, enclosing and opening up that allows a single entity to emerge from myriad individual perceptions, as if the urban landscape were carried over into the interior as well.

Matthias Sauerbruch and Louisa Hutton's mode of thinking and acting is defined by what they once described as "free thought and free form" – and I would add that it also encompasses the courage to engage in experiments that always include the future, too. They go the extra mile, offering something more, and it is precisely that "something more", to quote Theodor W. Adorno, that goes beyond a building's utilitarian value.

58

Dirk van den Heuvel

# Letter to Berlin

**59**

Dear Louisa and Matthias

A long and also much overdue answer to your question. It has been on my mind ever since it landed on my virtual doormat: What to say about the "turn of the century" and the current state we're in? It's such a big question, and the events of last year have been simply overwhelming.

Alison and Peter Smithson famously stated that they were after a "rough poetry" in their architecture, achieved against all odds, "dragged out of the confused and powerful forces which are at work".

But after Brexit, after Trump? Too often, I have to pinch myself in the arm to assure myself that all this is real and not just another bad Hollywood film.

What follows is written as a letter to the two of you. Thinking out loud. An academic piece felt out of place. Also, when I started working on the text, I realised that I've been affected by the past events much more than I'd like to admit, from the pandemic lockdown situation to the unnerving news-feeds on the American elections, culminating in the storming of the Capitol. This month, we had national elections in our country, in the Netherlands, and the political parties seeking a generally white Europe and aiming for a programme of "de-Islamification" gained almost 20 per cent of the votes.

How did we get here? To the point of accepting rampant xenophobia as the new normal? How is it that our very own leaders are aiming to dismantle democracy and the rule of law? And this is just our bubble in the West. What about current developments in Hong Kong? Or in the streets of Myanmar, at the university campuses in Turkey, the ongoing siege of Idlib in Syria? In Australia, a mining company recently destroyed the Aboriginal burial sites at the Juukan Gorge – caves that are 46,000 years old, their traces of human occupation now irrevocably lost in the search of iron ore.

How is one to drag poetry out of this brutality? How to remain optimistic?

## What might be lost

Architecture sits somewhere between the small things of everyday life – how you walk into a room, set a table, decorate the window – and the big events of history, of relentless modernisation and political power play. And these days, in an admittedly escapist mode, I'd much rather focus on those small, pleasurable things than the harrowing developments that unfold on the omnipresent screens we carry with us all day long, and which keep on bring-ing disruption into our rooms, while we're sitting around the table, or lying in bed watching a film.

This moment in 2021 seems so different from 1989, when the Berlin Wall came down and the Iron Curtain was lifted, events which took everyone by surprise. Without a single shot being fired, let alone an act of war, the process of reunification of East and West in Europe had begun.

I remember this vividly, as I'd visited the divided city just before. I was a 21-year-old student in Delft, and had joined a group excursion to Moscow and St Petersburg (then still Leningrad). Instead of flying home directly to Schiphol, we'd planned a stopover in Berlin. The experience of communist paranoia had made me averse to visiting East Berlin. Instead, I was happy to explore anarchistic Kreuzberg and the latest IBA projects. At the Kultur-forum, I had my first encounter with the supreme control of steel and glass, stone and space, as delivered by Mies van der Rohe at the Neue National-galerie. Also, I was deeply impressed by the phenomenal landscape architec-ture of Hans Scharoun: the Berliner Philharmonie, and the Staatsbibliothek in particular.

Naturally, my opinion had been influenced by Wim Wenders' *Himmel über Berlin*, in which Scharoun's library figured as one of the main sites for the film's protagonists, with Bruno Ganz in the lead role as an angel who falls in love with a trapeze artist. A feeling of melancholia for what might be lost permeates the whole film, especially the opening shots: a moving, flying camera that pans from room to room, person to person, trying to capture fleeting, everyday thoughts of worry, love and aspiration, while in between we hear Peter Handke's poem softly read and half-sung by Ganz:

*Als das Kind Kind war,*
*War es die Zeit der folgenden Fragen:*
*Warum bin ich ich und warum nicht du?*
*Warum bin ich hier und nicht dort?*
*Wann begann die Zeit und wo endet der Raum?*[1]

## A new promise

The Staatsbibliothek is like a friendly giant. Due to its irregular geometries, it resists a conventional reading of its architecture – no typologies to rely on, nor codified decorum. Instead, it evokes associations with geological formations of other times, far removed from the trauma of the machinic and massive destruction of the Second World War. Beyond cynicism and nihilism, it offers another space, one that achieves a double gesture: to restore some form of continuity while also suggesting the possibility of a new beginning in order to try to recuperate the human and cultural values lost, first under the regime of Wilhelm II, and then under the Nazis.

When comparing the Philharmonie and the library, the interior spaces of the former are much more dramatic and spectacular in their architectural articulation. But the Staatsbibliothek comes with a delayed, lingering impression, since its architectural experience works through the body and its senses rather than the directness of the visual. The slow way in which the space of Scharoun's library unfolds when you enter its interior and climb the generous flights of steps, moving along the wide galleries and the quiet plateaux of study spaces, is nothing but the orchestration of a majestic spatial immersion, certainly something I hadn't experienced before. I'm from Holland after all, and Dutch buildings have to be light, small and efficient given the soil conditions and the limited resources available.

In 1989, the sculptural volumes of the Staatsbibliothek dominated the still empty *terrain vague* between the Kulturforum and Potsdamer Platz, with the Wall and its watchtowers in the background, along with the little yellow test train that was part of the propaganda project for the magnetic M-Bahn. And as I remember it now, as far as the eye could see, the muddy ground was occupied by the illegal "Polenmarkt". Even though the Wall hadn't come down yet, Polish citizens were somehow already able to travel to the West, which led to a spontaneous and surreal kind of bottom-up capitalism by the people.

A cascade of moments of liberation followed, big and small, as if years of blockage had finally found relief. The USSR broke up, and the Cold War era and the threat of atomic war became nothing but an awful, fading memory. A wave of optimism engulfed Europe. In the 1990s, the miserable Thatcher years were left behind, a young Tony Blair blazed his way to power with Cool Britannia in tow – that was before he would join Bush Jr in support of the 2003 invasion of Iraq. In South Africa, Nelson Mandela was released in 1990, after 27 years in prison, and the country's apartheid system was soon to be abolished. The internet took off, bringing about a new global culture. When laptops were a new thing! And mobile phones became massively available. A new sort of light, carefree and mobile way of living was within reach. And crucially for a gay person during those years, the deadly disease AIDS was succesfully contained with new medicines and therapy. A new party culture emerged, of which Berlin would become one of its centres. Optimism and freedom reigned. At least, that's how I recall it, a general feeling of freedom, progress and new opportunities.

61

Shortly after the Wall had come down, I would eagerly return to Berlin to make up for not having visited Mitte, Unter den Linden, Schinkel's masterpiece the Altes Museum, the futurist Fernsehturm, and the barren but astounding Alexanderplatz, from where Karl Marx Allee takes you out to Friedrichshain and further. To walk or bike onto Alexanderplatz, empty, disfigured, unfinished, and to simply undergo its vast, expansive scale was one of the most exhilarating experiences I've had. I can't quite put it into words, but for sure, such an experience was possible only after the old regime had gone and Berlin had been transformed – almost overnight – into a city of new promise.

## Riding the waves of market realism

Yet this is not the whole story. In much the same way that Reyner Banham developed two opposing accounts of the 1950s in his renowned "Stocktaking" essays – one discussing "technology" and the other following "tradition" – one might write a parallel history of the 1990s that runs counter to liberal victory and salvation.

The triumph of liberalism over communism was famously celebrated by, among others, Francis Fukuyama, who declared it the end of history, since the ideological wars appeared to be bygones. Yet even then, signs of other emergent forces, the "clash of civilisations", were clear enough to see that such a provocative claim was built on hubris, not analysis: the ensuing Yugoslav wars should have sounded alarm bells as they were based on a mix of rekindled nationalism, racism and Islamophobia, just as the Tiananmen Square tragedy in Beijing – also in 1989 – signalled the imperial reflexes of a new world power on the rise.

For architecture and city planning, the end of the Cold War had two immediate effects. First of all, in the West, the welfare state system as an overarching framework to regulate spatial planning and distribution of resources was to be definitively dismantled. And second, free-market enterprise went hand in hand with a new conservatism and populism, which had been on the rise since the late 1970s. In the Netherlands, the new geopolitical condition induced an unprecedented alliance between liberals and social democrats, a new kind of progressive market realism, that was translated in the forward-looking architecture of SuperDutch (is this still a household name?). Whereas the conceptual, neo-modernist approach of a handful of offices was celebrated in the international media, quite another architecture flourished, too – a historicist pastiche architecture which flooded the towns and suburbs of the Low Countries.

Architectural criticism transformed into architectural branding, and I myself was glad to escape into the archive, to embark on a *recherche patiente* together with Max Risselada to retrace the sources of a socially responsible architecture, while the general opinion was that such an effort had desperately failed. Speaking to crowd-filled halls in Delft, Rem Koolhaas posed as the prophet of neoliberalism. In search of new opportunities, he castigated the welfare state for its gross incompetence, while mercilessly bashing Team X, Aldo van Eyck and Herman Hertzberger for their moralistic humanism. Jaap Bakema's work was simply ignored.

Viewed from the Netherlands, the direction of architecture and planning in Berlin seemed a mixed bag, to say the least. Rather than embracing the new freedom, the response to the new, post-welfare state reality culminated in the regressive doctrine of so-called critical reconstruction, based on the city repair approach developed during the IBA years in the early 1980s. As is well known – I hardly need to explain this to you! – the critical reconstruction approach largely based itself on a defensive kind of typo-morphological orthodoxy of closed urban blocks, and strict control regarding height, façade design, maximum volumes and setbacks. Controversially, the reactionary mood also directed the decision to demolish the socialist Palast der Republik, designed by Heinz Graffunder, chief architect at East Germany's Building Academy, to make way for the revisionist reconstruction of the Berliner Schloss, the former Baroque residence of the Hohenzollerns, which opened only last December.

## Radical contextualism

It was against this mixed mood of conservatism and new freedoms that your project for the GSW Headquarters appeared, which (as if by magic?) managed to bypass the dreary rules of the Berlin *Senatsbaudirektor*. It signalled optimism and cheerfulness, and how the language of modernism and the 1950s could be recharged with flair and conviction – quite in opposition to the desire of so many revisionists to erase the recent architectural past.

In hindsight, the clear and colourful composition of discrete volumes around the existing tower block read as an announcement of the later, more intricate projects: in particular the attitude of generously including, responding to and building on existing structures (as mundane as these might be), and the extraordinary undulating, polychromatic façades, which are intelligent climate sensors and regulators at the same time. Modernist tabula rasa and transparency are reworked into a method of layering and weaving.

What the GSW Headquarters project demonstrated above all is that another kind of contextualism is possible, more versatile and intelligent then historicist, typo-morphological orthodoxy.

This is also how I would like to understand the Smithsons' call for a rough poetry drawn out of the forces at play. Such poetry is too often misread as Brutalist provocation, as *épater le bourgeois*, whereas it actually concerns a practice of radical engagement and contextualism. Perhaps ecological or environmental would be better terms – since contextualism as a term seems too close to post-modernist semantics as propounded by Charles Jencks and Colin Rowe.

**63**

It's also from their search for a new radical contextualism that the Smithsons were great admirers of Scharoun's work. They even had him invited to one of the Team X meetings, prompted by their appreciation of his proposal for the Hauptstadt Berlin competition of 1957–58, where Scharoun had been awarded second prize and the Smithsons, together with Peter Sigmond, third. They included Scharoun's "Stadtlandschaft" proposal in their manifesto-like booklet *Urban Structuring*, in which they showed more of their Berlin projects, while talking about the newly imagined Berlin as an undivided, "open city" for an "open society". It's from Scharoun's concept of urban landscape that his projects for the Philharmonie and Staatsbiliothek would spring.

Much later, in the 1980s, the Smithsons will finally find the words to describe the qualities of such an urban landscape, when they reconceptualise their proposition for a New Brutalism as Conglomerate Ordering. Their appreciation concerns a topological architecture that goes beyond the sheer visual, which "harnesses all the senses", offering "pleasures beyond those of the eyes". An architecture that cannot be reduced to diagrams, that is elusive and "hard to retain in the mind", for it's characterised by a "variable density" and "irregular geometry". And yet, according to the Smithsons, when moving through the spaces of such conglomerate order, one can almost instinctively find the way in and through these spaces, which are "an inextricable part of a larger fabric".

## Sensing colour

What can one say about such pleasures beyond the visual and the generous and unapologetic use of colour in your projects? I would like to offer a few speculations here. Thinking out loud again.

My first proposition is that the use of colour is a crucial element in the contextual approach that you develop. It's part of an architectural strategy that addresses how one might operate in the new unstable situation, post-welfare state, now there is no larger framework that guides the architectural project. Under the impact of new technologies and globally connected economies, what we keep calling "city" is now a ubiquitous condition, a continuum in which the architectural project is an intervention that can regenerate and impact transformation, insert new values, a strategy of both continuity and renewal.

But how to read the use of colour? One sees suggestions that point to codes, signs or signals. There are associations of camouflage techniques, with examples of dazzle painting patterns, and clouds of pixels in glazed brick. The colours also come as dressing, mediating between decoration and the tectonics of a building, which is the "natural" and accepted place of colour in terms of the theory of modern architecture since Semper.

Within the modernist tradition, the visual is associated with the rational, the conceptual and intellectual, the project of enlightenment. But the eye is also a body part, and a sensor. From seeing to sensing is a shift that parallels the shift from the typological city of the 19th century to the emergence of urban ecologies in our 21st century.

64

Just as the eye and the brain are parts of the body, colour is a thing of the body first and foremost. I would therefore suggest that colour is not merely visual in your work – it is to be sensed rather than be seen. Even when the application of colour is abstract in terms of compositional techniques (serialist, strictly geometrical, repetitive and modulated, coded), it resists abstract, rationalist concepts of architecture, space, time and matter. Colour is sensed corporeally, to be experienced while moving around and within the building, with the light being reflected and absorbed in ever-changing ways.

Visiting the projects, it becomes clear that the use of colour is highly contextual, not just in the sense of fitting in or creating a contrast, but in terms of patterns from which an experience of immersion and recognition is constructed. This is also how your buildings take up their places in the larger urban fabric, and how one has to approach and navigate them. They might blend in like a chamaeleon, and then "emerge" from the fabric as a gestalt from the larger pattern, to create an event, invite engagement, mark a place, a point of orientation.

In such moments of individual recognition, the passer-by also owns the building, if only for a brief moment. Through daily routines and multiple visits, such brief moments build up into experiences, and the building and its colours, materials, textures affix themselves into the memory of tourist and local citizen alike. Such immersive contextualism gives way to a new kind of openness and multiplicity, in terms of experience and inhabitation.

## Creatures of optimism

A last thought for now, still unfinished it seems. In combination with the "weak" geometries of undulating volumes and the rhythms of softly bent and staggered façade systems, your buildings appear as creatures with a life of their own. Paradoxically, they are set apart from their context, while also engaging with it in a new way, a double gesture once again.

In your book on colour in architecture, you included an "incomplete glossary" for a possible manifesto on colour. Referring to Scharoun, one of the terms you list is indeed the German word *Wesen* – which you translate as "being" – to explain how a building should be exactly that, a being or creature, as well as a way of being in the world.

The notion of a building as a creature triggers many associations and resonates with today's ecological thinking, which seeks to connect a human and humanist perspective with more inclusive approaches to the environment. Today, ecological thinking holds a promise to be able to go beyond the relentless destruction of our environment. I would say it also denotes the still powerful agency in and of architecture, as a creature is something created, while also a creative force itself in place making. Such creatures present a rhythm of their own, and so – like Handke in reverse – time breaks up for a moment, and space begins, for recuperation and optimism, still.

Dirk
Amsterdam, 31 March 2021

1    "When the child was a child / It was the time of these questions: / Why am I me, and why not you? / Why am I here, and why not there? / When did time begin, and where does space end?" Part of a poem written by the Austrian author Peter Handke in 1986 for Wim Wenders' *Der Himmel über Berlin* (1987; released in English as *Wings of Desire*).

**65**

**66**

Kieran Long

# The Trenches of the Culture Wars

## Architecture and Context in London and Stockholm since 2000

My turn of the century was spent in London, a city I once felt I would never leave. In 2000, London was in the ascension. In the decade and a half that followed, statistics and laurels would catch up with the energy that the city had enjoyed at the turn of the millennium: London passed its record population and became by some measures the world's most popular tourist city. It became the home of embarrassing amounts of clean, semi-dirty and filthy money, laundered through its volcanically overpriced residential property market. It (again, by some measures) overtook New York as the world's financial centre. The 2012 Olympic Games were the most visible peak of its powers, marked, for me, by the surreal pomp of David Beckham racing down the River Lea in a speedboat, his hair flying behind him as he held aloft the golden, Barber Osgerby-designed Olympic torch. I remember watching it on TV, thinking of the mountain of old refrigerators that had stood on the banks of that same river just a few years before. London had transformed itself.

Someone who works at the Greater London Assembly once told me that when Ken Livingstone became mayor of London in 2000, the London Plan was still projecting a shrinking population, continuing the trend that had begun in the 1940s. What changed? As remote a feeling as it seems today, the late 1990s and early 2000s were a consensual time for urban policy in the UK. Tony Blair and Richard Rogers (Blair's urban tsar and later chair of London's architecture and urbanism unit under mayor Ken Livingstone) made a seductive pair, encouraging people back to inner cities, creating new mayors, advocating for investment in infrastructure and an architecture of density. The National Lottery funded several "grand projet" cultural buildings, the London wave of which was started by Herzog & de Meuron's Tate Modern in 2000 and extended to major new works of architecture in every major cultural institution in the city. Gambling funded London's bread and circuses.

The year 2012 was, of course, also the moment London began its descent. It was bigger, richer, more popular than ever, but then would come the 2015 election and the Brexit vote the following year. For all its glitz and wealth, London had no real answer to the way the rest of the United Kingdom saw the world. The crazy property prices, a surrender to international capital, and the provincialism of national politics meant that the position it had earned for itself could not be maintained.

Reading Sauerbruch Hutton's words on cities, it is clear that London and Berlin have shaped their subtle and serious attitude to the contexts of architecture. The London they remember is that of the 1990s, just before the ascent I describe above, where the city still had considerable areas of vacancy and dereliction, docklands and industrial zones with no real plan. Berlin retained some of that character much longer, not least because of the urban lacunae formed by the division of the city between east and west. These post-industrial cities are their playground, and their work thrives in these conditions. They are surely right to characterise London and Berlin as hugely important historical cities that nonetheless have whole swathes that are not considered "heritage". There is a freedom in these grey areas. In conversation, Sauerbruch Hutton describe their early work at the AA, working on ex-industrial and abandoned sites. Today, the city of Berlin forms one of their muses and topics, and the chaos and abandonment that even now characterises the city is the territory in which they feel comfortable.

**67**

If a sense of vacancy and looseness characterised London and Berlin in the 1990s and early 2000s, it was even more common to a great many smaller cities in Europe. Berlin-based academic and curator Philipp Oswalt's *Shrinking Cities* exhibition in 2000, and the books that followed, documented the phenomenon in excruciating detail. The project channelled Bernd and Hilla Becher in their dispassionate documentation of thousands of abandoned places, buildings, streets and towns.

In retrospect, and despite the authors laudable aims, the *Shrinking Cities* books did not escape feeling like a kind of catalogue of future actions. In-between spaces, derelict buildings, places of unclear ownership: all this felt like a territory of potential, a topic for architecture. But abandonment and liminality meant different things in different cities. In both London and Berlin, in-between, semi-abandoned sites were plentiful, hiding next to roads and railways, occupied or even contaminated by out-of-date industry, simply being used as surface car parking. In London, escalating land values made small projects viable for smaller investors, and, for a while, good things came out of this. Think of the one-off houses of Caruso St John or David Adjaye from this period, or the small-scale housing projects of Steven Taylor of Peter Barber Architects. The transitional economy of London in the late 1990s allowed good architecture to happen on unlikely sites. Architects were channelling Alison and Peter Smithson and the Independent Group, making similarly sensitive observations of the qualities of London that resided in its poorer quarters, particularly East London.

But all this was a double-edged sword. Architects made good work, but this conversion of "potential" into elegant, contemporary living space was complicit with a trajectory that wanted land values to rise, pricing the poor out and rewarding speculators, both landlords and ordinary homeowners, betting on rising values. Architects cannot be held individually responsible for this, but they found no way to significantly resist it either.

Some critics of a generation older than myself saw loss in the sanitisation that came to places like East London – banal new housing created for imaginary middle-class people, replacing the dust and grit of stonemasons' yards, the honest dilapidation of the junk heap. The psycho-geographers were disappointed. Their strain in writing about cities is basically elegiac. They want to wander the streets to detect the lingering signifiers of things past. East London, even post-Olympics, remains one of the great places in Europe to do just that. However, the phenomenon of drastically increased income inequality in London has turned out to be a much greater threat to its coherence and greatness as a city. The urban strategies of maximising "potential", densification and finding value in the rough worked, but they also helped to set in train a tide of gentrification that would create a polarisation that is now the fundamental dynamic of the public conversation that architecture currently faces.

In 2017, I moved with my family to Stockholm, a city that is, perhaps surprisingly, in the throes of a culture war partly being played out via debates about architectural taste. There was a general election here in 2018, and it was striking how much of the political discourse bore upon the built environment: safety in public spaces, the "uglification" of Stockholm through the demolition of historic buildings, and campaigns against individual building projects were all hot-button topics polarising the electorate. Architects themselves are not especially visible in this debate. While the debate about London's development certainly sees architecture as a symbol of a broader financialisation of the city's fabric, architectural style is seldom seen as a problem in itself. In Stockholm, the public conversation about the city is based on judgements about images in the newspaper, examining architecture as a visualisation and finding it ugly or beautiful, right for Stockholm or not. The sides in this debate are sharply drawn, and political in their nature.

Stockholm is the first city I have lived in that thinks of itself as more or less complete. The historic, inner city *inom tullarna* ("inside the gates") has, broadly speaking, retained its 19th-century character, with perimeter blocks and the grids they produce still predominant. Add to this a completely preserved medieval (and later) old town at its heart, and Stockholm is one of the most coherent urban environments in Europe. There are fewer gaps, lacunae and places of opportunistic "potential" here than in London, so its transformation must be more deliberate.

The historic character of most of the inner city is not complete. Several significant modern interventions, including large-scale road infrastructure that cuts swathes through the fabric of the city, are just as much part of the character of Stockholm. But by far the most traumatic 20th-century change to the city was the demolition of Klarakvarteren, the historic commercial heart of Stockholm that once occupied part of the Norrmalm district. This large-scale destruction of a historic quarter was undoubtedly brainless, and it coincided with inner-city interventions across Sweden in the 1950s and '60s that betrayed an arrogant and misplaced belief in car-based consumerism as the future for cities. Klarakvarteren was a place of diversity and intricacy, with buildings from many different centuries housing shops, hotels, small industry and craftspeople, the press and media, as well as entertainment and leisure. The area was cleared and replaced by modernist planning of large retail stores at ground-floor level and offices above. There are some modern buildings of imposing and civic character, the most prominent being Peter Celsing's Kulturhuset. But for all its virtues, Celsing's monumental cultural building (which would later serve as a kind of model for the Pompidou Centre) could not replace the culture that was lost in the demolition.

The tearing down of the old Klara quarter is interesting because it has caused a kind of trauma that seems to be inherited and gathering power. Its political significance has increased in recent years as right-wing political parties link preservation of old buildings to continuity of Swedish identity. They also use the apparently incomprehensible tastes of modern architects to create scepticism among experts and artists, setting popular taste against the taste of elites. Sixty years after it happened, the Klara demolition stands as irrefutable evidence of the inhumanity of modern planning. Popular campaigns have emerged and achieved results in electoral politics at the city level, and have begun to interfere in the planning system. A notable feature of the most recent general election was that so many parties campaigned on issues related to architecture, planning and public space.

The highest-profile target for politicians in Stockholm was a single building: the proposed Nobel Centre, a museum and cultural centre for the Nobel Foundation. David Chipperfield won the competition for the centre in 2014, but despite having full funding and most of its planning permission, construction of the building was cancelled in 2018 after an extraordinary public campaign that involved far-right politicians, wealthy private citizens (who wanted to preserve the views from their own balconies) and even the king. There was nothing democratic about the public "debate": it was a symptom of a culture war, the reckless exercise of extra democratic influence by people claiming to speak for "the people". Representing international, intellectual elites and with funding from some of Sweden's richest individuals, the Nobel Centre was to be built on a prime waterside site facing some of Stockholm's most expensive housing. It was the perfect target.

The attack on the building was about culture and aesthetics, but was also driven by some of the same dynamics that elected Trump and sent Britain out of the European Union. The rise of populism creates a new critique of architectural aesthetics that is difficult to deal with. It is a relief that Sauerbruch Hutton succeeded in building a tower here, in the south of Stockholm, without facing significant public opposition – perhaps because the building is just "outside" the inner city. It sits in the strange context of the Hammarby Sjöstad development: an exemplary low-energy urban quarter built in the 1990s around a historic industrial area. Stockholm One, as the new tower is called, conjures 35,000 square metres of space from a sloping, rocky site

**69**

between an elevated road and a tram track. For most Stockholmers, the building, completed in 2020, is experienced as a gateway to the city from the south. Its three-dimensional form tapers towards the base, its overall form never quite meeting the eye squarely. The tower is best seen from a moving car, as this enables the viewer to enjoy the colourful gables alternating with the long, sober façades. It is beautiful and ambiguous, having turned a leftover space into a site for a new symbol of the city. Bold, too, in having created a scale shift, a sudden upward momentum to the place. It is a building at the scale of infrastructure in a part of the city that is a strange mix of stadia, arenas, viaducts and benign modern suburbs.

The trajectory I describe above, from Blair's London to the divisions of contemporary Stockholm, is my own. But it has made certain the feeling that the fragile consensus that briefly existed in the 1990s between politics, the development industry and architecture has been profoundly shaken. This has remade the context for the profession. If I were to be hopeful, I would say that there is potential in this. Architecture must declare its cultural allegiances, for no anonymity is possible in a debate that is so polarised. Architecture is challenged to find meaningful connections with history and culture, without historical parody, and with an ethical responsibility towards social justice and the environment.

It is a time once again to set out the arguments that began in the vacant, underused parts of 1990s London and Berlin. These were places of irrational beauty, of chaos, of visual juxtapositions that reflected the mix of the cities and inspired an underdog pride in their citizens. These are the cities we need, places that reflect the profoundly hybrid reality we inhabit, that create a sense of our place in a world wracked by climate crisis and calls for justice from those too long excluded from the public realm.

70

Anh-Linh Ngo

# Landscapes of Logistics

Venice is pure appearance, as the saying goes. Like all clichés, there is
a grain of truth in it. This is, however, not simply about the seductive world
of illusion conjured up by the lagoon city's magnificent façades and laby-
rinthine alleyways that enthrals even the most jaded traveller. In a more
profound sense, more profound than we generally care to admit, it is about
a reflection of the politics and the economy of Venetian society. To quote
the philosopher and urbanologist Wolfgang Scheppe, we are looking at the
aesthetic reification of societal conditions: "When the abstract principles
of social, political and economic relations – such as division of labour –
are manifested in concrete form, they can be perceived viscerally and
explained via these concretions. The conditions that define the production
of space are thus legible in the space itself."[1] Viewed from this vantage
point, architecture and the city are the imprints of a society, which conversely signifies that the aesthetics of space is by no means extraneous
or superimposed.

In the transition to modernity, however, a momentous change took place both in Venetian culture's self-image and in its modus operandi: the unity of form and content – that is to say, of Gothic society's internal and external values – dissipated during the Renaissance, as Scheppe notes, drawing on John Ruskin. Art and architecture became part of La Serenissima's regime of impressive display, in which architects assumed the role of branding experts commissioned to convey Venice's long-standing economic power as a "world trade centre" by creating ostentatious façades. Venice's political influence was largely rooted in its trading might, which the city always deftly expanded with great strategic skill. In addition to the extension and defence of maritime routes, this included a systematic expansionary policy into the Venetian hinterland from the early 15th century on. Domination of the "terra firma" was not only important for provisioning this sea-facing city, but also contributed to managing and redeveloping the water basin through infrastructure projects that were needed to mitigate any risk that the Venetian lagoon might silt up completely. At an early stage in their history, the Venetians had already honed an awareness of the changes that their territory was undergoing. They needed to defend their city against the lagoon, which at the same time provided their livelihood and thus had to be preserved, come what may. Full of ingenuity and self-confidence, they set about diverting rivers, building canals, constructing dams – in essence: remodelling the entire landscape.

At a fateful point in history – after Christopher Columbus' landfall in America and after Vasco da Gama had opened up the southern sea route to India around the Cape of Good Hope in the late 15th century – that self-confidence had even led the Republic of Venice to devise plans to convince the Sultan of Cairo to build a canal through the Isthmus of Suez. With this gigantic infrastructure project, as Ludovico Centis recently recalled in *ARCH+*, Venice sought to defend its dominance over maritime trade against the emerging seafaring powers.[2] Even though the plan of 1504 was eventually abandoned and came to be implemented only in the colonial context of the 19th century, it testifies to Venice's strategic thinking and very early recognition of the global connections between politics and economics.

Despite such foresight, Venetian efforts to control nature, some even spanning centuries, were stymied by insufficient knowledge about historical geological and climatic changes – knowledge that had been lost in the mists of time, or rather under layers of sediment and enormous volumes of water. For archaeological studies show that in Roman times, the Venetian lagoon was divided into plots of land and used for agriculture. The findings revealed "that Venice, contrary to the legend carefully cultivated from the 9th to the 13th century, had not been founded by people forced to flee the mainland to escape barbarian incursions in the 5th century, but that the city came into being in the struggle against rising sea levels". Venice thus serves as evidence for the idea "that climate change has always influenced urban planning".[3]

Elsewhere, Wolfgang Scheppe dispels another legend, namely that Venice is a natural ecosystem endangered by anthropogenic influences: "Contrary to what environmentalists and nature lovers believe, Venice's lagoon owes its continued existence to a social order. The wish to forever fix as such a geological state reached in the Middle Ages transforms the natural space into a cultural landscape created wilfully by the authorities – a landscape which is dependent on a strict policy of water control, and which seeks to influence the natural water flow on a grand scale. The lagoon is therefore a highly artificial construct."[4]

In order to transform this absolute artificiality of Venice into a quasi-natural state that could be symbolically exploited, every aspect of daily life was gradually banished from the city. "Paradoxically, it was only in 1846, with the construction of the first railway bridge to the mainland, which provided the necessary infrastructure for industrialisation, that Venice became an island: an island of pure signs. [...] The bridge established a separation between abstract and physical production by isolating an old town on one side and an industrial city on the other. Venice has since disintegrated – like most major European cities – into the increasingly uninhabited representational realm of the historic centre and an agglomeration of dormitory towns, shopping malls and industrial zones that sprawl across the Po Valley."[5]

There is no better way to describe the duality of Mestre and Venice. As a result of their physical separation, both parts of the community embody the contemporary conditions of the globalised city in its purest form: the aggressive commodification of history, identity and location on the one hand and, on the other, the equally aggressive transformation of the globalised hinterland into a landscape of infrastructure and logistics that, through its productive forces, secures the value of the symbolic capital enshrined in the purportedly authentic historical centre. The paradox now is that one part has become uninhabitable as a consequence of speculation and spectacle, and we have long since made ourselves at home in the other part: in the landscape of logistics. Everyday life, having been forced to make way for the representation of the old town, is now flourishing in the globalised hinterland, of all places. Mestre is the everyday living city that Venice cannot ever be again.

I would like to approach Sauerbruch Hutton's M9 Museum project against the backdrop of this historical development: is it concerned with the inevitable extension of spectacle to the mainland, a process already in full swing with various large-scale projects, or does it represent an essential step in the reclamation of everyday life in Mestre? The direction the project will take depends largely on the society that has made Mestre its home after being driven out of Venice. If the first tendency prevails, that society will sooner or later make itself homeless again. If, on the other hand, local society pursues the Situationists' idea that everyday culture offers the only way to salvage life that had previously been abandoned to spectacle, it will find an ally in Sauerbruch Hutton's grounded architecture.

For the Situationists, everyday life, which they viewed as a sequence of individual situations, was the antithesis of the "society of the spectacle". In order to escape its clutches, people were to be empowered to reconfigure their alienated lives once again through situation-specific interventions. Similar approaches were also developed in architecture. Cedric Price and Alison and Peter Smithson, for example, endeavoured to create an architecture of enabling. Everyday life is central to such an approach; architecturally speaking, this entails reacting to the situation as-found rather than to functional concerns, while, in terms of the city, atmospheric cohesion becomes more important than functional segregation.

Sauerbruch Hutton's M9 Museum project in Mestre also adheres to this context-sensitive principle, in that it offers specific architectural situations and urban atmospheres to constitute Mestre as a cultural and social locus within a landscape of infrastructure and global logistics that the Veneto has become. Ultimately, globalisation simply signifies that we are more intimately interwoven with all aspects of the world than ever before. Faced with

**73**

this situation, resisting spectacle, which in turn is merely a reaction to the generic globalised city without providing a genuine response, is the most daunting challenge for contemporary architecture. In the face of populist, anti-globalist tendencies, architecture, along with society as a whole, must find a response to the question of how we can construct an identity that is not focused on formulaic categories, but instead takes account of societal dynamics and global interconnections.

One potential architectural response to this dilemma of identity policy can be seen in the site-specific interventions that make the new M9 quarter an architecture of enabling in the best sense of the term: an architecture that allows us to feel at home in the present, having been expelled from the "paradise of cities", as John Ruskin called Venice. Instead of nostalgically mourning the lost paradise, contemporary architecture is confronted with the noble challenge of contributing to the logistics landscape and simultaneously charging it with culture. As a result, architecture and urban space can become far more than a three-dimensional aesthetic concretion of society: their impact can indeed reflect back onto society and transform it.

1  Wolfgang Scheppe: "Realabstraktion und Fassade. Zur politischen Ökonomie der 'Stadt der Gesellschaft'", ARCH+, no. 204: Krise der Repräsentation (October 2011): 8.

2  Ludovico Centis: "Das Land teilen. Venedig, Suez und das infrastrukturelle Denken im frühen 16. Jahrhundert", ARCH+, no. 239: Europa. Infrastrukturen der Externalisierung (July 2020): 179.

3  Ibid., p. 177. Centis refers to the publications by Wladimiro Dorigo: Venezia origini – fondamenti, ipotesi, metodi, Milan 1983 and Ernesto Canal: Archeologia della laguna di Venezia 1960–2010, Verona 2013.

4  Wolfgang Scheppe: "The Ground-Rent of Art and Exclusion from the City", ARCH+ (English version): The Property Issue: Ground Control and the Commons (April 2018): 16.

5  Wolfgang Scheppe (see note 1), p. 10.

Veronica Simpson

# Architecture as Acupuncture

One of the most significant tropes of late 20th- and early 21st-century urban regeneration has been that eye-popping statement buildings can serve to trigger cultural and economic rebirth in cities whose glory days are often long gone or have yet to be imagined.

Frank Gehry and his Guggenheim Bilbao have the dubious honour of spawning the myth that a single architect and a singular architectural gesture can perform an act of heroic aesthetic acupuncture, unleashing latent energy and dynamism to an ailing organism and restoring it to peak economic and cultural health. What is often overlooked is that the arrival of Gehry's Guggenheim in 1997 was just one part of an ambitious, Basque government-led economic and cultural programme that included significant investment in Bilbao's education and technology sectors and a major upgrade to its transport and tourism infrastructure. Underpinning all of this was an aspiration to deliver architectural excellence that included commissioning a new airport by Santiago Calatrava (one of his more modest, elegant and efficient structures) and an underground train network with stations designed by Norman

Foster Associates. So, although it has come to be emblematic of Bilbao's success as a world-class tourist destination, Gehry's building was possibly more the cherry on the cake rather than the cake itself, for which it is usually mistaken.

In the two decades that followed, many sought to replicate the "Bilbao effect", seemingly confident in the belief that the larger and more international the architect's reputation or "name" and the more flamboyant the building, the greater its chances of success.

That has rarely proved to be the case. Calatrava's wildly ambitious City of Arts and Sciences for the economically depressed eastern Spanish city of Valencia possibly stands as the nadir of that kind of "build it and they will come" thinking. Stunning photographs of his space-age, curving structures still proliferate online, but when I visited in 2014 – only eight years after completion – the opera house lay empty and derelict, having lost all of the white ceramic tiles that had comprised its dazzling cladding, and only half of the "city of science" was still open, the rest of it barricaded off from the public.

France also fell for the idea of ambitious cultural / architectural acupuncture for its failing post-industrial cities, with regional departments commissioning a series of striking contemporary art galleries that usually involved architects from elsewhere, as showcases for their art collections. From the two examples I have witnessed, it seems that the more flamboyant or unusual of the pair – the luminous and alien-looking Louvre Lens art museum, completed in 2012 by Japanese architects SANAA – has had less success in endearing itself to locals or visitors than Lacaton & Vassal's FRAC Nord-Pas de Calais (2015), a gentle refurbishment of an old boat warehouse on the site of Dunkerque's port.

Why might that be? Perhaps because authenticity is one of the key ingredients in urban and architectural regeneration. This entails a willingness on the part of both client and architect to anchor their vision – aesthetic, civic and programmatic – in something that offers not only meaning, but also relevance and sensory delight for the proposed neighbourhood, as well as for those who might be tempted to visit. As the Finnish architect and theoretician Juhani Pallasmaa states: "I see architecture as the defence of the authenticity of human experience."

True to the Finnish spirit of collective endeavour and clever husbandry of resources, Pallasmaa's words resonate with Helsinki's own culturally-led regeneration project of the last six years. Having famously rejected the Guggenheim's offer (along with its heavy price tag for the use of their brand and collection) to leverage the city's cultural clout with a new statement building bearing its name, the Finns decided to deploy their reserves more wisely. They have restored and transformed an existing Art Deco cinema into a contemporary art space (Amos Rex, by Finnish architects JKMM); invested in new underground stations (designed by ALA Architects); refurbished a much-loved modernist landmark, the Helsinki City Theatre; and made their "statement" new building one dedicated to improving the lives of Helsinki's citizens: the Oodi, a remarkable new library, community and makerspace, also by ALA Architects. The final flourish is the launch of Helsinki's own contemporary art biennial (originally scheduled for 2020, it will now take place in 2021). Most significantly, the biennial will not be located in a new landmark building, but on one of their precious and unspoiled islands.

Further, its key themes and benefits will be to highlight environmental issues, encouraging visitors to embrace nature and the joys of being off-grid. That is nothing if not authentically Finnish.

Helsinki is not a city in need of economic rescue, however, and neither is Mestre. It is already a stable and solvent dormitory town, home to many of the workers who keep alive the extraordinary global tourist attraction that is Venice, just a fifteen-minute train ride away. It is (or was before the 2020 pandemic) the most densely populated town within the Venice commune, also housing workers for the nearby docks and petrochemical industries of Porto Marghera. But, unlike Helsinki, Mestre has an image problem: while it may boast a number of budget hotels whose prices are increasingly attractive to Venice's visitors, inducing them to eat or sleep here, it has little else that they are likely to remember. This is something the local community, as represented by the Fondazione di Venezia, aimed to address in its proposal to develop a cultural district that included a museum dedicated to Italy's 20th-century history. The international competition launched in 2010 for the design of the museum project was won by Sauerbruch Hutton.

Part of the appeal of their design was its holistic treatment of the site. Once home to a 16th-century convent (the Convento Santa Maria delle Grazie) that was later appropriated for use as an army barracks, the area had been walled off from the town for more than a century. The architects chose to make a north-south connection across the convent courtyard, forming a new public route that links the museum buildings to the wider street network, with an additional east-west link that now enables circulation around the shops and cafés that occupy both new and refurbished buildings. As part of Sauerbruch Hutton's proposal and remit, the convent itself has been restored and reincarnated as the hub of a new, creative, tech-friendly quarter that enlivens not only the ground floor with its bars and small shops, but also the upper floors of its central courtyard, which has now become an all-weather public piazza thanks to its hovering ETFE parasol.

In this way, the M9 project achieves another of the key characteristics of successfully regenerative urban schemes: it reveals a city, or an aspect of the city, to its citizens anew. This might more typically be a stretch of previously neglected or unlovely riverfront, as was the case with the Guggenheim Bilbao, built on the unfashionable side of the River Nervión, on the site of the city's run-down former dockland and shipyards – or even London's Royal Festival Hall, which materialised in 1951 along the then grimy and uncelebrated south bank of the Thames, to be followed almost half a century later by Herzog & de Meuron's inspirational power station refurbishment: Tate Modern (2000). With their M9 scheme, Sauerbruch Hutton have returned to Mestre's citizens a part of their own historic city centre, along with some new public space.

The role of architectural spectacle in any successful regeneration project is debatable. But where there is an image problem, it is certainly useful. The arrival of Will Alsop's Peckham Library – a tall, inverted L-shape of a building, its library floors cantilevered out over the entrance trunk, and topped by what looks like a flying saucer and giant "library" lettering on its roof – changed the way the citizens of Peckham saw their area, and the way Londoners regarded it, too. It had previously been viewed as a no-go area, flanked by hugely problematic post-war estates, and riven by a noisy, polluted arterial highway running from central London to the south-east. The building went on to win the Stirling Prize, and slowly but surely – thanks also to its continuing affordability – the area has become a magnet for young creatives, enjoying new galleries, expanded cultural institutions and a vibrant, independent food scene.

In order to have an impact, the M9 Museum therefore had to stand out to a certain degree. This it certainly does with its colourful, ceramic-tiled façades. The pair of buildings may appear somewhat alien compared with the potpourri of structures around them, but the M9's unusual geometric forms and vibrant colours are not a case of dazzle and shape-making for their own sake: the tiles' unusual mix of reds, pinks, ochres, greys and creams are all tones that can be found in the stone, brick and predominantly rendered buildings in the towns and landscapes of the region, while the strategy to divide the body of the museum into two structures rather than a single, larger one effectively reduces its architecture to a scale that is in keeping with the surrounding urban tissue.

Furthermore, the experience of being in the building delivers an enhanced perception of the location, for both locals and newcomers, through unexpected views and vistas that build on the sensory richness generated by form and material.

As you ascend the impressive staircase – enjoying the tactile wooden banister, and the shifting patterns of shade and sunlight that pour over the rugged, concrete walls from the series of large and variously oriented windows and skylights – there are wonderful moments that reveal the recent and historic urban fabric of Mestre in a new way: a long, diagonal slice of window that follows the gradient of the stairs, framing first the façade of the smaller *Administrativo* building opposite and then the surrounding rooflines; a second-floor teaching space (the *Aula Didactica*) whose large and generous window set deep into the exterior wall presents the rich terracotta and ochre townscape, like a painting that illustrates the city's recent history; the top-floor landing between stairs and gallery further captivates with views deep into the building that fall away from you on either side; finally, there are charming bird's-eye perspectives panning over the heterogenous cityscape, offering views across the streets from the top-floor lounge area and roof terrace.

For a new building to truly connect with its environment, the activation of memory – aesthetic, kinetic and folk memory – is crucial. Louisa Hutton and Matthias Sauerbruch see the city as a palimpsest: what Aldo Rossi called an "urban artefact", made of its evolutionary layers. Architecture, says Sauerbruch, "embodies the memory of past, present and future" – words taken from an enriching series of conversations published recently in an issue of *Bauwelt* dedicated to Sauerbruch Hutton.

In this way, the materials used should not be spurious choices but the result of a consideration of ancient or modern skills and relevant materials. Many people (not architects, perhaps, but city planners and ambitious mayors all over Europe) mistook – and continue to mistake – the use of dazzling forms or façades as a crucial aspect of Gehry's regenerative fairy dust. They are wrong. Gehry's choice of titanium tiles for the Bilbao Guggenheim was inspired by the site's shipbuilding past, evoking the welding of metal plates onto curving prows – though, of course, he also knew how they would capture and reflect light from the river.

For M9's architects, the decision to use ceramic tiles was entirely congruent with Italy's history of architectural ceramics, extending way beyond Roman times. The life-affirming balance of delicate and vibrant shades reflects both the artistry and craftsmanship for which the Venetian region is famous. They are also part of the scheme's inherent sensuality, as described by Louisa Hutton in the same *Bauwelt* issue: "The application of colour to con-siderably smaller-sized elements means that as you get closer to the building, and parts of one's own body are perceived in relation to those of various bodily-sized pieces of the building, there is much more opportunity for cor-poreal entanglement."

That haptic experience of "corporeal entanglement" along the reinstated and revived streetscapes is quite likely a factor in the success of this new quarter, whose cafés, courtyard and generous public seating areas have become all the more vital during the coronavirus pandemic. However, while these new public spaces and facilities have outperformed expectations, the museum – even before 2020's lockdown measures were implemented – apparently did not.

Maybe it is of no consequence how splendidly sensory or authentic you make a building if the exhibits inside it are ephemeral and digital and, ultim-ately, predominantly engage with you on an intellectual level. Maybe the reason people return to the Guggenheim Bilbao, the Royal Festival Hall or Tate Modern again and again is their ever-changing displays, the contents over-whelmingly tactile and immersive, and authentic in their evocation of human history – in its particulars as well as its universals. But all of that could be altered with a change of policy and pricing designed to increase local access, with a desire to redeploy the national narratives and themes of the exhibitions within a more collaborative, personally tailored and engaging framework – one that examines people's own relationships with their place of birth or work. The digital nature of the exhibits could even prove to offer an advantage – by allowing greater dialogue between the objects inside the museum and the local audience. Such a strategy, along with an inspired series of events that address the local population in particular, could help to bind the museum into Mestre's identity.

The final piece of alchemy that ultimately determines whether a well-designed landmark building is loved or not lies in its programming. In this case, happily, there is plenty of scope – both in the architectural envelope and the narratives it frames – for positive evolution.

**79**

# 80

Jean-Louis Cohen

# A Joyful Complexity

One of the most vivid architectural impressions I experienced in the wake of Berlin's reunification had to do with the closer connections that were suddenly possible between neighbourhoods that had previously been hermetically sealed off from each other. One could now walk from the Hansaviertel's modern slabs to the socialist-realist mini skyscrapers at Strausberger Platz by way of Unter den Linden. However, if there is one building that I would say symbolised the era of system change – *die Wende* – in Berlin's architecture, it would be the extension for the GSW Headquarters, commissioned to Sauerbruch and Hutton in 1991. Located in the middle of the Friedrichstadt, just two streets away from the legendary Checkpoint Charlie, and engaged in a dialogue with both the Springer office tower, which in its day had been provocative, and Leipziger Straße's prefabricated residential high-rises with their panels, it became a watchtower for something that could be thought of as a third Berlin, erected along the scar tissue of the two half-cities inherited from the Cold War. With its curving form, it displayed an unusual suppleness in reaction to the hegemony of the right angle that in no way shared the poetic values with which Le Corbusier had imbued it. The play of colour across its façade panels broke with the drab greys that had been de rigueur on both sides of the wall for decades.

This addition, wrapped as if in a mortal embrace around the existing tower, recalled earlier attempts to inject radical designs into the neighbourhood, starting with OMA's 1980 competition project at Kochstraße / Friedrichstraße, at the time in stark contrast to the post-modernism that infiltrated the early activities of the nascent *Internationale Bauausstellung*. The original tower looms like a silent witness in the axonometric drawing on a black background that indicates how the residential units are to be embedded into Berlin's urban fabric. Delving further back into earlier chapters in the city's history, it would be hard to ignore Alison and Peter Smithson's entry for the 1958 *Berlin Haupstadt* competition, in which the current GSW site is slotted into the tracery of circulation routes in a plan punctuated by tall buildings not dissimilar to the one that would be completed by Sauerbruch and Hutton in 1999.

Since that stroke of brilliance – in an almost literal sense, given the building's luminosity – they have continued to explore in greater depth the themes that were already present *in nuce* in that Berlin building, in the process proposing their own discursive interpretation of their designs and built work. The "family tree" that concludes the second volume of their *archive* – a compendium of the studio's production – bears eloquent witness to this. To continue the arboreal analogy, the extension of its branches stimulates the expression of new propositions, while at the same time reining them in to some extent. I shall nonetheless be so bold as to venture down some of the paths suggested in that array of dense paragraphs.

Starting with the GSW Headquarters, a focus on ensuring that buildings were anchored in their site became a constant in Sauerbruch Hutton's problem-solving, although without producing the kind of crippling mimesis that holds form to be simply the product of contextual parameters. Inserting curvilinear forms into the generally stubbornly orthogonal grid layout of European cities involves a desire for singularity, manifested at ground level by the appearance of an object with unexpected volumes that can be perceived in its entirety – even if that is rarely possible at first glance – by adopting a kinetic or even cinematic approach. In this context, the design strategy is informed by theories of the urban picturesque, for the projects maintain an implicit relationship with the irregular configuration of the medieval squares so dear to Camillo Sitte. Through inverse contextualisation, the strangeness of the supple forms, the façade rhythms and the colours of these newcomers suggests a new reading of the pre-existing fabric within which they are placed by drawing attention to its scales, volumes and textures. The intruder does not internalise a relationship with a location's previous history, but instead articulates it by entering into a conversation with its predecessors, framed by the interstitial spaces between the curving volumes and the mass of the surrounding context. The ripples radiating outwards may encompass much more than just the surrounding buildings in the case of recently constructed neighbourhoods. Thinking along these lines, the context for the ZAC Claude-Bernard office building in Paris (2008–12) is produced by the red-doored, blue-and-white commuter trains speeding past on nearby tracks, along with the heavy traffic on the Paris ring road that runs immediately adjacent to the site.

At first glance, the curvilinear contours of the architecture create a link between buildings that have very different uses and forms. The Photonics Centre in Berlin-Adlershof (1991–98) and the Cologne Oval Offices (2007–08) play on the juxtaposition of two volumes that serve as a mirror and context for one another. Other buildings – which in a sense remain unattached like Marcel Duchamp's "bachelor machines" – may unfurl their curves in

**81**

relation to the building line, as in the Saint-Georges Centre in Geneva (2004–12), thus adding intensity to a tranquil urban façade, or may conjoin them with orthogonal forms, as in the Kinetik office building in Boulogne-Billancourt (2009–13), where this duality reflects the heterogeneous functions accommodated within the building. In larger projects, the curvilinear motif tends to become an urban system in its own right. That holds true for the looping form of the Federal Environmental Agency in Dessau (1998–2005), with a constantly curving outline that meanders and folds back on itself as it delineates the space of a linear atrium. In the case of Hamburg's Ministry for Urban Development and the Environment (2009–13), the architecture in a sense becomes discursive in the spirit of Enlightenment "architecture parlante", with its zigzag outlines, which in the design plan appear to form a jaw on the verge of devouring the university buildings along the site's north edge.

The "organic prisms" that have punctuated Sauerbruch Hutton's output over the past thirty years thus pick up the architectural debate that burst onto the scene during the 1940s, when the Museum of Modern Art in New York presented the *Brazil Builds* exhibition, sweeping away the timidity about non-rectilinear geometries that had hitherto defined the mindset of the primarily European or North American founders of what is generally known as the "modern movement". Precedents can be found in the sinuous forms of Oscar Niemeyer's apartment block in the centre of Belo Horizonte (1954–59) and his Copan Building in São Paulo (1957–66), yet Sauerbruch and Hutton are not simply uncritical inheritors of *carioca* architecture. In these two Brazilian towers, reinforced concrete flooring sections cantilever out from the structure, functioning as sunscreens that accentuate the sense of horizontality and underscore the buildings' monolithic heft. Nothing like that figures in the examples I have described above, for the very different climatic conditions in São Paulo's tropical environment mean that these buildings must take refuge behind a watertight façade. The lines traced by their curves are not continuous but are instead segmented into panels and shutters with a chromatic configuration that, in turn, accentuates the undulating outlines.

**82**

Characteristic factors of this kind, which are, in a sense, external and give rise to a dynamic tension that shapes the building envelope, as if echoing certain hallmark curves from Erich Mendelsohn's architecture, are reinforced by internal characteristics that respond to the brief, in a sense exerting a centrifugal force. In projects developed for institutions or administrations, these, for the most part, involve deploying modular, serial units, such as offices or small conference rooms, in conjunction with larger meeting rooms and common spaces that give the buildings their identity. This twofold effect arises as a result of abandoning any kind of pre-established typology. The structure and modules are reinvented for each design brief, even if some superficial resemblances might lead inattentive observers to conclude that there is repetition rather than variation. The two most eloquent examples of this a-typology are the architecture schools designed for the universities of Melbourne and Toronto, with almost antithetical components that seem to accentuate the differences in their didactic programmes.

Having abandoned the safe haven of reassuring experiences afforded by typological catalogues, design inventiveness is crystallised in the routes around the architecture, as is eloquently demonstrated in the Experimenta building constructed in Heilbronn between 2016 and 2019. Visitors can explore the galleries and the various sections inviting discoveries about prodigious achievements in science and technology by advancing along an ascending spiral route, defined by stacked segments that give the building its form. The robust steel structure – which combines with a central concrete core that coincides with the spiral's vertical axis – together with the trusses of the façades, create spaces that offer scope for any subsequent reconfiguration of the museum's displays. This is a reformulation of a principle first expressed by Le Corbusier in his 1928 Mundaneum project, subsequently inverted in Frank Lloyd Wright's 1944 Guggenheim Museum design and revisited by Rem Koolhaas in his 1992 Jussieu library project.

While fairly unforgiving imperatives tend to constrain the design of office buildings, museums offer more fertile ground to imagine an architectural *parti* by means of the dialectic established between galleries, with their need for strictly controlled environments, and the circulation routes through and around the buildings – which in most cases play a key part in defining their monumental impact. The narrow footprint of the Brandhorst Museum in Munich (2005–09), squeezed up against the edge of a small plot in the Kunstareal, left little scope for anything but a linear configuration, which took the form of a foyer and straight-run stairs bathed in fine natural light that lead to calm, serene galleries. Another linear stairway connects the levels in the M9 Museum in Mestre (2014–18); it is skilfully inserted into the site around the Convento Santa Maria delle Grazie, where a diaphanous covering set above the cloister has transformed it into a location that can accommodate creative activities. In contrast to the strict liaison of Heilbronn's form with its circulation path or the way in which the galleries fundamentally define the form of the Munich museum, M9's architecture explores and enhances heterogenous resources – be they existing massing, low-lying volumes clad in ceramic tiles or the gallery crowning the ensemble, its saw-tooth skylights reminiscent of the ones created above former barracks to house Sauerbruch and Hutton's Berlin offices. The diagonal passageway separating the two new volumes is another trope of the picturesque-oriented approach cited above. The project's contradictory complexity was condensed into the *Oxymoron* installation, presented in the Corderie exhibition space at the 2018 Venice Biennale of Architecture, in which the façades' opaque polychromy became translucent and almost faded.

**83**

As in most of the projects devised or realised by Sauerbruch and Hutton, colour is a constituent component of M9. In this particular case, the ceramic cladding combines tones that meld with the atmosphere of this Venetian city in an approach that strongly resembles critical mimesis. However, that is more of an exception than the general rule if one takes the various "chromotopes" into account, to use the eloquent neologism proposed in the second volume of *archive*. The deployment of colour in the interior or on the façades is not determined by sterile systematics but is much more reliant on research into relevant substrates. As a function of the different projects, the colours may unfurl on façade glazing (Dessau), louvres (Photonics Centre), pivoting-sliding sunshades (GSW) or ceramic rods (Brandhorst). The strategy for the K House in Munich (2013) involved finely detailed pixellation of the façade to conjure up a kind of velvety appearance. Through all these means, colour becomes a medium for defining the public space in which these buildings are set. Yet it has nothing in common with Le Corbusier's polychromy, derived from painting, or Friedensreich Hundertwasser's audience-pleasing colour mash-ups. It is more reminiscent of poet Paul Scheerbart's prophecies of a world of multicoloured glass replete with marvellous potential and of the strategies utilised by his friend Bruno Taut for the streets of Magdeburg and the houses in his Berlin *Siedlungen*.

Since the GSW Headquarters refurbishment, issues of sustainability have played a decisive role in projects developed by Sauerbruch Hutton, who have succeeded in tackling them undemonstratively and without overblown rhetoric. The spectrum of principles and technologies employed in this context has continued to extend ever since, ranging from passive strategies, incorporation of experimental materials or spatial inventiveness to active solutions that include specific features to shield façades or to enable air and water circulation. Just as modern 20th-century architecture mastered novel construction techniques and teased new poetic forms of expression out of them, starting with reinforced concrete (I am thinking here of Auguste Perret or Oscar Niemeyer), these projects reject any kind of exhibitionism about sustainability. They reveal how climate protection issues have been "assimilated", in Swiss psychologist Jean Piaget's sense of the term, which denotes the integration of a new object or situation into an existing reality.

In his beautiful book *On the Mode of Existence of Technical Objects*, French philosopher Gilbert Simondon gave an account of the process whereby an object that is initially "abstract", as it is composed of heterogenous solutions, becomes "concrete" when those solutions are integrated into a unified form; he alluded to the first automobiles, which were simply motorised coaches, to exemplify the first point, while the second category was represented by later, more aerodynamic vehicles. In this spirit, successive projects by Sauerbruch and Hutton crystallise a complex way of thinking into forms whose youthful joyfulness and apparent simplicity are deceptive, for they result from integrating the major challenges of our era into buildings that each display a distinctly new personality.

84

Florian Heilmeyer

# Into the Great Wide Open

Educational fields in the states of Western Europe and North America are in flux. Over the past thirty years, pedagogical concepts and educational trajectories and formats have proliferated. The three major trends of our time – capitalisation, globalisation and digitisation – have exuded enormous pressure to reform schools and academies, along with libraries, museums and other extra-curricular educational facilities. This pressure is, in fact, a good thing, as it has also helped a number of somewhat dormant reform concepts from the early 20th century to break through – together with their associated spatial manifestations. By now, in 2021, the entire educational landscape appears more diverse, pluralistic, open-minded and liberal than ever before – and this is, of course, clearly reflected in those spaces in which learning takes place. The most important tendencies are a general openness and increasing flexibility of use – both of which encourage creative appropriation – that have affected all major learning typologies.

## Expanding schools and academies

Europe's schools were certainly already changing before the OECD began conducting its international PISA studies. However, the shift has gathered significant momentum since then: longer school hours that even extend to what are known as all-day schools simply had to transform the school spaces to expand from mere "teaching and learning" spaces into a much wider set of "living" spaces. Nowadays, school premises are used not only for assistance with homework, sports and additional tutorials, but must also afford scope for leisure activities, meals, quiet time or rest. This calls for larger premises with new types of interior and exterior spaces, ideally with parts that can be used flexibly throughout the day.

Such an extended brief means that traditional school designs, organised around corridors with rows of virtually identical classrooms, are now heading for extinction. Circulation zones in particular offer enormous potential for multifunctional use: generously sized corridors offer accommodation for spatial modules that can be assigned flexibly for class or group work; wider staircases become auditoria; and a variety of events can be set up in foyers or sports halls with movable tribune elements. Cluster schools are slowly becoming today's standard, with a core of smaller room modules that can easily be restructured into various new combinations over the course of the day by flexible walls or similar spatial means. Such schools increasingly resemble universities and academies, thanks to their considerably expanded spatial programmes.

In universities, on the other hand, a twofold opening up can be observed both on the urban and the interior scales. Open spatial landscapes may seem less revolutionary in universities than in schools, as the tradition of studios combined with work spaces and the provision of unprogrammed intermediate zones have been established here for some time. The most radical example of this to date appears to be the architecture faculty in Nantes by Lacaton & Vassal (2009). Here, the entire building is made up of such "spaces for appropriation": the users of the building find a set of empty, open and robust spaces of various sizes and heights that present a spatial puzzle they have to solve according to their own, changing needs.

This functional flexibility within has been supplemented by a second trend: the wish to offer greater public access from outside. Although universities have long proclaimed this intent, practical efforts to turn their buildings into public venues such as event halls, public libraries or open cafeterias are more recent. Functionally clearly defined rooms tend to be reduced to a precisely programmed core, while other activities spread out into adjacent flexible zones, such as corridors, staircases, platforms or halls. Typologically, it is no longer at all clear what such buildings actually are. In essence, they mostly appear to be spatial relatives of the magnificent Kulturhuset in Stockholm (1971) by Peter Celsing, with its wide-open, functionally diffuse spaces. Recent examples of such buildings include the Town House for London's Kingston University by Grafton Architects and the EPFL Learning Centre in Lausanne by SANAA.

## Expanding libraries and museums

Compared with schools, the evolution of libraries has been going on for some decades, as the pressure exerted by digitalisation and the ensuing crisis for printed material has, of course, hit the core idea of the library both harder and faster. The continuous democratisation of the library as an institution is a development that can be traced back through almost the entire 20th century, but is one that accelerated dramatically in the 1990s. It has found its most radical redefinitions to date in Toyo Ito's Sendai Mediatheque (2001) and, a few years later, OMA's Seattle Public Library. Like the new

schools, these libraries have developed into places for more than just learning; with their multifaceted public programmes, they have instead become
venues that embrace everyday life and offer users an agreeable visit, making
them very popular despite the decline of book borrowing. Again, we find an
ever-growing zone of "ancillary" and flexible spaces that can accommodate
a wide range of events, exhibitions, courses, teaching and educational
programs — and, of course, in the age of commercialisation, also spaces
for consumption, retail and restaurants.

The new significance accorded to architecture's interstitial spaces could
become the most important difference between the 21st and 20th centuries.
In the past, the size and shape of most spaces were determined by precisely
stipulated activities. Perhaps it would be fair to say that we are now in the
throes of gradual defunctionalisation, of a new openness for architecture.
Similar tendencies can be found in new residential construction with its
multiply coded communal zones, cluster floor plans and gallery access to
the upper floors, as well as in designs for open office landscapes that are
currently replacing all-too-familiar cellular structures.

This also holds true for the museums of today. Former ancillary areas have
been steadily and considerably enlarged in this context as well, becoming
activity centres in their own right. Examples include the conversion of
Bankside Power Station in London into Tate Modern by Herzog & de Meuron
(2000). This exemplifies how even a building as hermetically sealed as a
power station can be criss-crossed by a diverse spectrum of routes that
maintain connections to the exterior, while encompassing myriad public and
semi-public spaces that are not just consumer-oriented, but also operate
as spaces for appropriation with functions that are either ambiguous or with
multiple codings.

Two of Sauerbruch Hutton's most recent projects also explore this territory,
if in very different ways. The M9 in Mestre, completed in 2019, is simultaneously a museum and an educational and event venue. The Museum District
comprises a number of buildings – most notably the now converted Convento
Santa Maria delle Grazie. Unfolding among the heterogenous architecture
of the immediate surroundings, its small museum piazza has become the
publicly accessible centre of the entire area. Passageways lead out from this
"piazetta" to the south and north through the newly covered cloister of the
former convent, which is now a covered outdoor space. Restaurants, shops
and co-working areas enliven the urban rooms that have been created.
Inside the museum, public areas – the mediatheque, auditorium, café and
museum shop – are located on the ground floor, fully visible from the street,
piazza and passageway. Thus in M9, the museum's spatial programme
extends beyond its outer walls, flowing into the adjacent urban fabric. This
seems to contribute largely to a new, expanded understanding of what
a museum can be today: the museum as an activity that is not bound to the
building's limits but is in many ways interwoven with the public realm of
the surrounding city.

Experimenta in Heilbronn, also inaugurated in 2019, likewise displays an
open relationship to its urban context. The new building is oriented towards
its older neighbour, a former warehouse structure in which the Science
Centre, set up as a private initiative, has been presenting exhibitions since
2009. With its floor-to-ceiling glazing, the new Experimenta opens up in
equal measure to three sides: the river, its older sibling as well as a broad
pedestrian and cycle lane that leads to a recently developed landscape

**87**

park. The restaurant and the impressively dimensioned Science Dome provide an edge towards the river. To reach the exhibition areas from the ground floor, a route spirals upwards; visitors circle the core of the building via escalators to end up on a generous roof terrace with panoramic views of Heilbronn and its vineyards beyond. On each floor, the helical route leads one through a series of large, polygonal foyers: these spaces for appropriation are flexible in function, serving as communication and learning points for everyone who weaves their way through the rich offerings of the Science Centre.

## Spatial landscapes for the 21st century

All of these architectural propositions – cluster schools, workshop universities, expanded libraries and open museum buildings – give us an inkling of the substantial changes that have been and will be happening in educational facilities. The boundaries of inner spatial landscapes must be renegotiated, along with their transitions into urban space and the borders of traditional typologies. There appear to be more and more similarities between museums, libraries, universities, cultural centres and schools. These typologies will need to be reconceptualised in the new century. New terms will be needed.

The Shed in New York, for example, designed by Diller Scofidio + Renfro and opened in 2019, describes itself simply as a cultural centre. A completely open structure comprising four two-storey halls stacked one upon the other, it offers a platform for all kinds of cultural presentations – screenings, discussions, exhibitions, theatre, dance or performance. The entire building envelope can be moved 80 metres on a rail system to cover a public square, and thus turn the ensuing 40-metre-high empty volume into a truly grand space for appropriation that can be addressed on any of the four levels. It is an enormous cultural machine that, incidentally, references – just as the Centre Pompidou and the Kulturhuset did some forty or fifty years earlier – the concept of a Fun Palace as had been developed by Cedric Price for and with the theatre director Joan Littlewood.

It remains to be seen, however, whether we as users will be able to cope with an architecture that frees itself from the all-too-narrow spatial prescriptions of the functionalisms of the 20th century. We may, perhaps, finally be ready for such a Fun Palace after all.

Marco Biscione

# An Innovative Ensemble

Putting the project for the M9 Museum District into practice constituted a radical innovation within the Italian museum landscape and entailed rethinking the very concept of a museum. Towards the end of the last century, a new vision had already begun spreading internationally that set visitors together with the local and wider community at the heart of the museum's remit: museums are no longer simply focused on preserving and displaying exhibits, but instead have become active cultural agents that aim to serve their community in its cultural, civic and economic development.

The establishment of major cultural institutions in conjunction with iconic architecture has helped urban centres blighted by late-20th-century deindustrialisation to overcome profound crises. Reinventing themselves as cultural capitals, they have created cultural demand and tourism-based revenue streams. New-build projects have often become magnets in their own right, sometimes irrespective of the type of the museum.

Italy has long been renowned for its exceedingly rich legacy of museums that have taken shape over the centuries with historical collections at their core. This cultural heritage encompasses more than 5,000 sites, and the country has therefore been slow to embrace new visions for museums and their innovative potential as institutions. Only very recently have a few examples emerged that were designed with a view to forging such an intimate alliance between the buildings, their institutions and their context.

In this respect, M9 is currently Italy's most comprehensive and cutting-edge project; for the first time, a museum forms the nucleus of a regeneration strategy devised to foster development in a location such as Mestre, which could – to some extent – be seen as a paradigm of the country's most recent history.

The thematic focus in M9 is innovative: it is the first museum in Italy to tell the country's story over the course of the 20th century by concentrating on the transformations that have changed people's lives rather than on the broad sweep of history or major events (although these, of course, form the backdrop and foundation for this tale of the Italians). Every visitor who has lived through the 20th century will find their own past reflected in this narrative and will recognise a collective history. This form of historical account is inspired by the Anglo-Saxon concept of Public History, which breaks out of the specialist academic context to address the general public, helping to foster a shared civic awareness.

It is a polyphonic history recounted entirely through a multimedia presentation that is both immersive and engaging. As a digital, dematerialised museum, M9 eschews the type of exhibit that has hitherto formed the raison d'être of such an institution: works of art, objects and mementos. Here, the visitor dives into an experience that is provided completely in digital, multimedia formats. The relationship between visitor and museum is turned on its head. Without visitors, this museum does not exist; it appears in dialogue only when its audience actively engages with its content.

The entire project is interpreted and informed by the M9 ensemble's architecture, which gives expression to the museum's ambitious goals. The architects faced the daunting task of interpreting and making manifest the museum's essence and its remit. They had to devise a form that combines efficient spatial organisation with effective messaging, while also ensuring that the architecture does not upstage the displays. The building's role is to create an initial, fundamental encounter with its audience that encourages immersion in the museum's narrative.

The M9 ensemble has fully achieved its goals on that count, as both the architectural concept and the technical and cultural programmes have been co-developed with a focus on functionality and impact. The "black box" exhibition halls on the first two upper floors have been designed to create a completely immersive visit that draws visitors right into the multimedia experience. In addition, the expansive, light-filled stairways culminate in a large "white cube" exhibition space on the third floor, which provides an extraordinary, flexible, multi-purpose platform for the shows and pop-up events that form the backbone of the museum's cultural output.

The architecture has generally proved to be a magnet for visitors, greatly benefiting the museum's cultural programme. The spaces within the building (the foyer, the auditorium, the workshop and seminar areas, as well as the immense gallery on the third floor) have done more than simply provide an effective backdrop for the various projects (exhibitions, conferences, lectures, workshops, screenings, concerts). They also play an integral part in all of these activities and trigger responses from curators and artists alike, as demonstrated in an immersive video installation that was specially conceived for the museum by Fabio Massimo Iaquone. Projected onto the concrete walls in the stairways, it took viewers on an existential and metaphysical voyage that reflected on the relationship between humanity and the universe.

The container and its content form an indivisible, harmonious whole in the visitor's experience and imagination, with the container neither eclipsing the content nor remaining merely an anonymous and dispassionate backdrop.

## Building, museum, city

Ambitious and in certain respects visionary, the M9 project is rooted in the specific urban context of Mestre. The development of Mestre and Marghera in the 20th century as a residential and industrial complex is paradigmatic of the somewhat belated advent of the modern age in north-east Italy. In just a few decades, large-scale industrial units encompassing the whole spectrum of modern manufacturing (petrochemical plants, shipyards, port facilities) sprang up here, helping to forge the bedrock of Italian industry in the period known as the "economic miracle". Growing demand for labour in these enormous plants attracted tens of thousands of workers from all over Italy, who moved to the urban agglomeration with their families.

This sudden population influx resulted in a phase of unruly, unconstrained development without any master plan or zoning provisions and gave rise to sprawling urban growth that completely ignored the aesthetic and functional imperatives of urban development. M9's third-floor terrace offers a panorama of city that appears chaotic and random in terms of aesthetics, building mass and scale, as well as functional distribution. Over and above its own complexity, and as one of the largest urban agglomerations in the Veneto region today, Mestre also has a complicated relationship with the historic island of Venice, which differs from it in every respect: in its history, role, economy and culture. The various public consultation processes that have sought to achieve administrative separation over the years between Mestre and the historic centre underscore the tensions inherent in this dialogue.

**91**

It is specifically with a view to boosting development of this entire area that the Fondazione di Venezia, a banking foundation with local roots, has undertaken this ambitious urban regeneration project centred on a cultural institution, an innovative museum: a first for Italy. The site chosen for the museum – defined by the 16th-century former convent of Santa Maria delle Grazie and the former barracks (which was still owned by the military) – lies right at the heart of central Mestre, and for decades had cut off this sizeable central area from the surrounding city. The choice of location had a significant impact on the city, returning a previously inaccessible part of Mestre to public use.

M9 forms the nucleus of the project but encompasses much more than simply the museum. The M9 buildings have catalysed a broader intervention that includes restoration of the former convent and development of a location for retail and gastronomy. This makes M9 a multi-purpose ensemble that offers a range of cultural, recreational, entertainment and commercial services. The original project envisaged that the commercial and leisure activities would help the museum become economically self-sufficient; the idea was that this private-sector institution, which receives no public funding, would attain financial autonomy through ticket sales and rental revenue from the commercial units.

The key feature that led the architectural design by Sauerbruch Hutton to be selected in an international competition was its proposal to "open up" this area to the city, rather than creating a new "limited access zone" in the centre, however fascinating that may have been. The M9 ensemble establishes relationships and builds connections: between different areas of Mestre, between the city and the museum, between a community and its history. It connects various functions (cultural and economic), it connects spaces, it connects people and it connects Mestre to an international context.

That is particularly true in that its scope and scale also make it significant beyond the frame of the Mestre / Venice area. In addition, the aim to present Italian 20th-century history goes beyond bolstering historical knowledge (and awareness) among Italians. Some of the vast flow of international tourism that has besieged the historic city of Venice will no doubt be redirected towards M9. As an innovative, state-of-the-art project, the M9 ensemble will attract international audiences who will experience a visit to the museum as an intriguing complement to their exploration of the historic islands.

The M9 project is therefore innovative, ambitious and visionary. But what has it actually achieved? Have results lived up to expectations? Taking stock more than two years after its inauguration, both positive and negative conclusions emerge. The difficulties encountered during this period, with the pandemic forcing the museum to close for more than a year, has meant that the museum has been slower to attract high numbers of visitors to help make the commercial units viable and thus sustain full financial autonomy. In addition, economic transformations affecting both urban centres and business models, shifting trends in consumer behaviour, and the boom in online commerce have all made it imperative to reconsider whether the district around the museum should continue to focus on retail outlets.

Against this backdrop, more time is needed to fully assess the outcome of the project and determine to what extent the museum can attract visitors and thus attain more broad-based acceptance. A series of systematic surveys of audience satisfaction after visiting the museum reveals very positive approval ratings; about 95 per cent of those asked are satisfied with their experience, would recommend the museum to others and intend to return. The average length of stay is 130 minutes. This indicates that visitors are becoming involved in the M9's narrative, interacting and engaging actively with the experience rather than consuming passively as they do in conventional museums.

An analysis of the relationship between the museum and the city is, however, also crucial in fully taking stock of the overall M9 endeavour. For many years, M9's construction site impacted on the city centre, and initial community responses to the project, which many felt was out of touch with local needs, were anything but enthusiastic. The museum's decision to move beyond the extremely local level disappointed those who expected that it would concentrate solely on Mestre's history. Although some concerns may linger when it comes to the cultural and economic side of the M9 project, the architectural dimension has nevertheless already unfolded its full potential and demonstrated its scope to forge connections.

The people of Mestre have enthusiastically taken possession of the areas around the museum, breathing life into them, strolling through them, visiting the district's bars and restaurants and filling them with energy. The square outside the museum became a new meeting place and a forum in which to gather (at least until the pandemic forced it to close), thus fulfilling one of the project's objectives by opening up spaces in this district for use by the local populace.

Against the backdrop of the somewhat ambiguous results for M9* as a whole, this cultural venture to create a multimedia museum of the 20th century proves to be replete with potential and new prospects. These have, however, been slow to take hold due to the unresolved relationship with a local community that still does not identify fully with the project, particularly as it has not yet established a robust national and international reputation. On the other hand, the architectural side of the endeavour, with its striking visual and functional impact, fulfils its role as a vibrant receptacle for cultural and urban regeneration initiatives. This magnificent polychromatic repository, which contains all the colours of the city, has already become the hallmark of the Museum of the 20th Century, as well as of Mestre.

* The Italians refer to the 20th century as the "Novecento" – hence the name M9 for a museum about the country's history between 1900 and 2000.

# 94

Eric Parry

# The Colours of Life and the Air We Breathe

Taking a broad view of the considerable output of Sauerbruch Hutton, I am particularly taken with two parallel but intertwined streams of thinking. The first is the deep-rooted concern over both the environmental performance and the sense of well-being their buildings induce – this includes at the larger scale the urban context, but also the intimate experience of the user on account of the high quality of light and air that is achieved in the most passive way possible. What is striking and impressive is that this has been an ardently held ethical position from the outset of their collaboration. The second is a rare and sophisticated attitude to the use of colour in their work, through which they have challenged the mainstream of contemporary architecture, both in Germany and internationally.

While I do not intend to dwell on biographies in this brief review, the roots of their practice are significant and interesting. Matthias Sauerbruch and Louisa Hutton began working together more than thirty years ago in London, where they shared the creative and exploratory architecture – avowedly anti the established professional scene of the time – emanating from the studios of the Architectural Association, where they were both studying for the AA Diploma. Thereafter, they mixed teaching studios at the AA with their respective engagement in London offices. Louisa worked for Alison and Peter Smithson for four years during a period when the commission for buildings for the University of Bath was underway, including its new School of Architecture and Building Engineering. This period was during the twilight years of the Smithsons' practice, but it was also an open door to a rich knowledge of the culture of architecture, art practice and urban planning in post-war Britain. The Smithsons' journey began in Newcastle upon Tyne, where they were both students and where Peter Smithson subsequently became a lecturer at the newly formed Department of Town Planning, along with rather overlooked figures like Thomas Sharp and William Whitfield. Alison Smithson was also a writer and a powerful mentor for gender equality, publishing *A Portrait of the Female Mind as a Young Girl* in 1966. The fact that she gew up in Sheffield provides a degree of circularity to Sauerbruch Hutton's Jessop West building in that characteristically northern city with its strong industrial past.

Just as the Smithsons produced a key building of the post-war years at the outset of their career with Hunstanton Secondary Modern School, completed in 1954, so Sauerbruch Hutton came to the forefront of architectural discourse with their Berlin headquarters building for the GSW, conceived in 1990. Following earlier student stints in various architectural practices in Berlin and his subsequent graduation from both the Hochschule der Künste in Berlin and the AA, Matthias joined the London branch of the Office for Metropolitan Architecture, founded by Elia and Zoe Zenghelis, Madelon Vriesendorp and Rem Koolhaas. He soon became an early partner to lead OMA's Checkpoint Charlie project in Berlin. With regard to the topics of colour and air, Matthias' familial connections are intriguing. Firstly, his father, Hans Sauerbruch, was an artist and Matthias grew up with an attunement to landscape and colour, as well as the smell and haptic qualities of the studio. Perhaps even more evident in his attunement to the anatomy of buildings is the work of his paternal grandfather, Ferdinand Sauerbruch, a leading surgeon of particular inventiveness and skill who early in his career developed the so-called Sauerbruch Chamber – a device to allow operations on the open thorax. This happened at a time when tuberculosis was having a profound effect on architecture, in that the importance of air quality and the consequences of segregation were being increasingly understood. Both are uncomfortable reminders of the recurrence of lessons learnt for today and the future of communicative space as a goal of architecture within its provision of a framework for social interaction.

My first encounter with a built work by Sauerbruch Hutton was a visit to the newly completed GSW Headquarters as a member of a judging panel. It impressed and touched me then, and I continue to hold the project in very high regard. It is not the physical evidence alone that left such an impression, but the dogged determination to succeed when so much had obviously been thrown in its path. Important, too, was the fresh use and consideration of both material and colour. The published evidence for the latter is no doubt a relatively small proportion of the studies produced. There are, for example, four compositional alternatives of the site plan, powerful, painterly, earthy oil pastels applied over precise architectural scaled plans. They indicate the way in which the proposal served as an urban receptor, reconciling, for instance, the older Junkerstraße in the raised glade of trees. Their spring leaf echoes the bands of green corrugated metal of the floating, three-storey ocular form resting above the gentle concavity of the Kochstraße building.

One of the early study models, strong and intuitive like the oil pastel drawings, is a collage of representational materials chosen to highlight the different parts of the building. The pre-existing GGZ complex is in cast plaster, the same material used to model the surrounding structures. The new, almost perfectly square elevation of the proposed slab adjoining to the west of the pre-existing tower is thin on plan, like an urban sail compressed into a subtle concavity. This is made of an acrylic block on which a lightly sand-blasted surface, with a textile-like composition of rectangles, suggests a luminous presence and hovers weight-defying over the pair of base buildings represented in carved blocks of dark timber. Implied in these choices is a structuring between earth and sky to which the colour and material palette directly corresponds. As built, the low-rise buildings remain dark. They are clad in a fired clay tile of quite substantial thickness, glazed in an anthracite grey and laid with expressed horizontal joints that emphasise the material stack, thus adding to the visual weight. These volumes are earth-related, like a tectonic plinth on a carpet of grey granite sets that literally runs though the entire ground floor as a landscape, drawing together the street and the south-facing court to the west of the site. The chthonic nature of these materials and spatial choices reach a resolution in the cave-like reception space that is dramatically top-lit with views of the towering structures overhead. The aqueous colours that bind the reception desk around the west corner pier of the older tower accentuate the sculptural massiveness of the ground floor in contrast to the perched architecture above.

The old tower was refurbished, cleansed and integrated into the new ensemble through the provision of a new lift core, half of which sits between the deep external columns on the west side of the existing structure, the other half sitting within the new west wing. The original building, a vestige of the post-war struggle for West Berlin's identity, was treated respectfully. Its muscular exoskeleton is highlighted in light grey, with the horizontal weave of the spandrels adding a darker tone. Seen from the east, the tripartite composition of new and old presents a muted grisaille of whites and greys. It was a clever decision to allow this palette to draw together the disparate elements and yet, at the same time, to celebrate the order of the new tall building, which displays a weave of white spandrels bound together by vertical metal ventilation grilles. The relative neutrality, in terms of hue, of the east side of the project is then contrasted with the massive canvas of the west-facing urban mask. With its innovative kinetic life reflecting the occupants' comfort, this elevation is both an urban billboard announcing the GSW with its city-social pact to provide housing and one of the leading environmental statements of its premillennial time. The west façade comprises 648 storey-high glass units, each of which is further subdivided by a trio of pivoting-sliding, perforated metal panels. With its combination of ten hues, varying from pink to deep earthen brown, it is like an urban-scaled Advent calendar of perpetual surprise. During the competition, the architects described this façade as echoing the warmth of the tiled roofscapes of a traditional city. Underlying this contextual resonance is a more painterly attraction on the part of Matthias and Louisa, particularly with reference to the base red: "The strong oxblood of Nordic timber houses, the intense vermillion on Japanese Temples, the soft pinks that define the city of Jaipur and those vivid pinks of Luis Barragán."

Although this well-travelled sourcebook indicates the breadth of possibilities, there is a clear discipline to create a limited palette. This follows historical examples such as those used by 17th-century Dutch painters – think of Rembrandt's severe use of hues and tones that range between deep shadows, fleshy complexions, textiles, sometimes red, and the glint of pearls and golden threads. There is enough difference between the dark panels and the Jaipur pinks to allow the essential warmth to glow in amorous excitement in the afternoon light.

96

One of the lessons learnt from GSW is the permanence of pigment in liquid-applied coatings. A fired glaze on terracotta, a ceramic matrix applied to glass, an interlayer of stained glass, or vitreous enamel all offer an enduring pigment. One of the earliest examples of Sauerbruch Hutton's applications of ceramic baked onto glass can be found in the combined Fire and Police Station for the government district of Berlin (1999–2004), close to the River Spree and Berlin's main railway station and within sight of the Chancellery. It is an inventive riposte to the relatively massive scale of GSW. Interestingly, both schemes succeed in part because of the integration of pre-existing buildings. The architects' earlier proposal for the Paternoster development in London (1989) took a similar and, at the time, rather exceptional approach to urban transformation – particularly when considered among the graveyard of propositions made by many of the foremost practices of the day – choosing to retain the barely thirty-year-old buildings by modification and addition.

The new building for the Fire and Police Station wraps itself around the five-storey fragment of a massive former customs office, making use of the existing single-banked corridor. Like the west façade of the GSW, the new element levitates here above the ground floor, enabling parking for police cars and fire engines alike. The subtle convexity in plan here contrasts with the concavity of the GSW, presenting a bold but simple statement that both delights and surprises with its provocative colour choices – and not only in the context of the plethora of doleful, boring police and fire stations in Germany, particularly from the 1960s and '70s. Unlike the heavy, well-built historic structure, the proportions are landscape-format in composition, both in the new building as a whole and in the polychromatic glass shingles that make up its skin. The complementary colours of red and green, the essential palette of the building, are difficult to combine. The result is successfully achieved through the gradation in hue across the entire building, the scale of module, the syncopation of the fifteen-glass shingle stack and the forty or so keys in length – making for a successful, chameleon-like metamorphosis from red / fire to green / order. A humorous irony for viewers (and there are many) of the long-running German crime film series *Tatort* is that in order to comply with EU colour codes, the police in Germany now wear a blue rather than green uniform.

While green, the dominant colour in nature, is strongly associated with restorative benefits, the colour also has negative associations and can be interpreted as threatening, even poisonous. The German *giftgrün*, for example, is variously translated as "bilious green", "acid green" or "toxic green". And art historians have dwelt on the use of this colour in paintings such as Édouard Manet's *The Balcony* (1868–69), where the emerald green of the balcony railings and the tight framing of the green shutters undoubtedly reinforce the sense of unease felt by the three figures emerging from the luminous black of the interior to observe the outside world.

With regard to the challenging combination of red and green, Vincent van Gogh sums up its potency when describing to his brother the palette he used for his painting *The Night Café* (1888): "I have tried to express the terrible passions of humanity by means of red and green … Everywhere there is a clash and contrast of the most disparate reds and greens."[1] To have chosen this combination is, on the one hand, obvious, but to have used it to such positive effect in this context is both audacious and intelligent.

The weave touched on earlier as a significant part of the east elevation of the GSW in Berlin was developed further in a subsequent commission for the

University of Sheffield in England: the Jessop West campus building (2005–08). The Y-shaped plan of this complex was generated by its location at a busy intersection, on the brow of a hill, as well as by the desire to create landscape spaces between its limbs. It was also informed by the architects' interpretation of the brief: to draw together three independent faculties into a single building in such a way that their spaces could intersect and share a social hub.

Depth of façade has been a characteristic of the projects described: the ventilating cavity of the west façade of the GSW is in the order of 100 cm; the glass shingles and the opening louvres of the Fire and Police Station some 70 cm; the visible build-up of the Brandhorst skin 15 cm; while in contrast to all of these, the surface of Jessop West is determinably flush, with depth implied by the composition of parts and the combination of hues and tones. Unlike some of the circular or continuous façades explored in other projects by Sauerbruch Hutton, the three legs of Jessop West allow for each to have a predominant colour: red, green and blue. The implied weave and combination of rectangular panels placed between or surrounding the fenestration units inevitably brings to mind the Op Art creations of a generation of abstract artists, such as Bridget Riley, but also the "Space", "Sky", "Masonry" and "Sand" combinations of Le Corbusier's colour keyboards produced by the Swiss wallpaper manufacturer Salubra in the 1930s and 1950s. The flushness of the façades that allows these painterly analogies to read so clearly with their subtle differentiation of reflectivity in the adjacency of materials also masks a layer of airways behind the surface. Where the site is acoustically challenged, there is the greatest attenuation of sound; and rather akin to the chimney flues within the party wall of tenement buildings, air movement within the faculty building is created by the stack effect through a matrix of voids. With Jessop West, I find myself applauding the response and clarity of the building in the context of an eclectic mix of urban remnants and architectural mutterings.

The adoption of an ambitious goal to create a naturally ventilated building was a design principle clearly established from the outset. In terms of the evolution of the project, the clarity with which this objective has been carried through, from site orientations to individual occupant control of solar shading and airflow, is an exemplar that should be a case study for students of architecture or indeed urban and interior design. The space on plan required to achieve these environmental goals – for instance, the great west façade, where a continuous solar chimney was deployed to draw air across the floor plates, and kinetic panels were installed to control solar gain and glare – would otherwise have succumbed to the fiscal demands of the developer. The long-term investment in lower cost-in-use has since become an essential part of building performance targets, and the GSW Headquarters will remain a pioneering building in this regard.

Sauerbruch Hutton have explored a wide range of sizes in their use of coloured modules in their buildings, generally responding to elements of structural dimension, but particularly fenestration. At the GSW, the hues that make up the palette of the west elevation are applied to the entire façade through the perforated panel system designed principally for solar protection. In the case of the Berlin Fire and Police Station, the scale relates to the height of the horizontal order of overlapping glass shingles, within which the transparent window openings take their place. At Sheffield's Jessop West, it is the weave of the vertical bars or warp elements that forms a combination of two hues of differing shade, occupying a rhythm of single- and double-height units drawn together by the horizontal stainless steel spandrels. At the Brandhorst Museum in Munich, the scale is reduced to that of a considerably smaller unit of fabrication, a pointillist mark almost, where the blind walls of the museum allow a continuous surface to be considered. It is a relief that the gravitas and wonder of the collection of art housed within the building have led to its relatively stable form in conformance with its orthogonal context.

The museum is conceived sectionally in three parts, whereby the lowest is sunken into the ground and receives top light through horizontal glazing located beyond the upper curtilage. The ground floor is made up of a sequence of spaces lit primarily from a strip of clerestory windows. This forms a strong horizontal order on the exterior, separating the upper floor from the ground level. The upper floor of the museum is predominantly top-lit through the roof to maximise the capacity of the internal walls to accommodate art – especially given the considerable scale warranted by contemporary art practice. The building is, as one has come to expect from the practice's work, an exemplar of passive energy use with particularly sophisticated heat-exchange systems that ensure a very stable environment at relatively modest running costs.

A part of this is the well-insulated jacket, over which a subtly psychedelic quilt creates a deceptively light, even levitational, ascending order, playing between the deep tonality of the base and the delicate warmth of the upper level. It is extraordinary to experience how heavily the horizontal emphasis of the neighbouring buildings sits in comparison – whether it be the balconies of the one or the brickwork of the other. The building elements that make up the mirage effect are simple and economic: they are principally square sections of extruded clay – 4 × 4 cm in size with a wall thickness of 9 mm – cut into lengths of 120 cm. This optimises strength and tolerance and is a well-established industrial process. Like the choice of dyed threads on the bobbin of a tapestry weaver, the colours create rich adjacencies in their possible combinations over the canvas of the building. The result is, in effect, an open mesh – applied over the weathering skin – that also uses the shadows created by the spacing of the square section bars. Additional variation is achieved by the folded backing skin, which produces a depth and weft to the whole and, with such capable judgement of colour, a sensational and ever-changing appearance.

As for air and colour, or environment and delight, Sauerbruch Hutton's response has been determined and coherent from their beginnings. The life-threatening environments humankind has created in the name of progress, and the harrowing consequences for the natural world, increase an architect's responsibility not only to design buildings that mitigate their inevitable impact, but also to provide newly designed environments that bring pleasure. This is not just a question of the materials used, but also the way the building behaves in use and indeed over its entire life cycle. By this relative measure, Sauerbruch Hutton lead a clear path in the application of integrated environmental systems, technological advances in manufacturing and responsive building management.

The question of delight – in this instance, through the use of colour – is a response to a dearth of serious consideration of this subject in architecture today. One evidence of this is the lack of any courses on the subject in schools of architecture – with very rare exceptions. Equally telling is that the history of the modern movement is enshrined in an archive of black-and-white photography, although in its European roots, colour was an essential part of its foundation. During my own academic tenure at the University of Cambridge (1983–97), I was fortunate to share my interest in colour with two eminent historians. One was Robin Middleton, a scholar of 18th- and 19th-century French architecture and author of an important essay on the influence of the early 19th-century polychrome campaign of Jakob Ignaz Hittorff, who subsequently used sophisticated chromolithography to support and popularise his arguments. The other was John Gage, who was working at that time on his seminal *Colour and Culture: Practice and Meaning from Antiquity to Abstraction* (1993), to be followed a few years later by *Colour and Meaning: Art, Science and Symbolism* (1999).

My hope, of course, is that this academic focus on the visual arts may now find a natural extension into the built environment, not least because its potent force can too easily be abused and needs to be part of a wider cultural discourse.

1   Van Gogh in a letter to Theo van Gogh, written 8 September 1888 in Arles. Translated by Johanna van Gogh-Bonger, edited by Robert Harrison, number 533, http://webexhibits. org/vangogh/letter/18/533.htm (accessed 5 June 2021).

100

Thomas Auer

# The Aesthetics of Sustainability

From the very beginning, sustainability has been inherent in the architecture of Sauerbruch Hutton. Resulting from their belief in the responsibilities of the profession, They have never considered sustainability as a mere "story" or something that engineers might add to their projects. Looking for an architecture of integration, Sauerbruch Hutton have always approached their designs from first principles.

"Sustainability" is a most misused term, but that does not mean it is wrong to use it or that the ideas behind it are not gaining in importance. As Matthias once said in an interview: "Despite all the inconsistency, misuse and clichés, I have not come up with a better term yet, but the question for us is how can a building also gain some of its appeal from the fact that it is designed to be sustainable? Can "sustainability" become the benchmark for a new aesthetic, just as "light, air and sun" were the leitmotifs for the modern movement some 100 years ago?"

In another conversation a few years ago, Matthias stated: "We have better insulation, better energy systems, smart grids and wind turbines on green fields – at the same time, we observe that these innovations seem to go hand in hand with a certain trivialisation of our surroundings. Obviously, decarbonisation doesn't automatically lead to added value in our urban or rural environments." In his opinion, it is the task of architecture to deliver both liveable and likeable atmospheres, as well as a light footprint on the planet in a new aesthetic instead of delivering "business as usual" veiled with a bit of technology.

In this context, the colourful compositions of Sauerbruch Hutton do indeed have quite some importance. After decades of exposed concrete, steel and glass, it was a relief for me to see architects produce buildings that are actually friendly. In this, however, their use of colour is neither just superficial decoration nor visual branding. One understands that it is the result of an intellectual discourse that is looking for sensuality within an architectural environment, and that colour is but one medium in their toolbox. Louisa states in a recent *Bauwelt* issue: "We are interested in sustainable buildings and in an architectural language that relates to this concern. [...] applying polychromy to just those building components that are instrumental in an ecological approach, we try to combine the scientific aspects of architecture with an appearance that is both empathetic and inviting. We try to nobilitate components that are normally seen as technical, possibly even embarrassing."

In our Transsolar brochure, we describe our own work as "the generation of a climate concept in which form, material, and mechanical systems are synergistic components of a well-orchestrated climate control system" – in other words, we write that we are aiming for "an environmental control strategy that is integral to the architectural concept". Louisa's statement thus confirms the intellectual foundation of our long-standing collaboration.

The ongoing search for an aesthetic of sustainability is a process in which various aspects of sustainability are becoming more – or in some cases less – important. In the works of Sauerbruch Hutton, one can see how priorities shift, adapt, grow and improve incrementally over time. I have chosen five of their buildings to illustrate this process. Although we actually collaborated in only one of these projects – the KfW building in Frankfurt – I have deliberately made this particular selection as it perfectly illustrates the continuous evolution of their work.

## GSW, Berlin

The GSW high-rise in Berlin was not only a central project for Sauerbruch Hutton. It was conceived at the beginning of the 1990s, when we also looked curiously and enthusiastically to London. Firms like Richard Rogers, Foster and Partners, Ian Ritchie and many more had developed an architectural language in which environmental considerations were an integral part of their architectural approach. Engineers like Buro Happold, who already had a close connection to Germany and especially to Stuttgart, Ove Arup, and individuals with smaller but equally innovative offices, such as Max Fordham, Guy Battle and Chris McCarthy, or Patrick Bellew (to name just a few), cultivated the idea of integrated environmental design. The modern movement had insisted on the intelligible integration of structural systems in the architectural expression of a building – the Munich Olympic stadia from the early 1970s perhaps representing a certain climax in this way of thinking. By the 1990s, the idea of integrated design was complemented with a discipline called "climate engineering", which was concerned with the design of environmental quality. So it was no longer just about equipment for heating and cooling, ventilation shafts, ducts and all the rest. Suddenly, engineers were talking about architectural elements such as façades, shading devices, thermal mass, chimneys for natural ventilation, and so on, as well as how passive systems could be hybridised with mechanical systems that were considerably smaller than those to which one had become accustomed. From now on, architects – at least those who were interested – had a partner with whom they could discuss an environmental approach to their designs.

During this phase, Sauerbruch Hutton won the competition and went on to realise the GSW high-rise in Berlin. With this building, they were making an important contribution to the future of the district of Kreuzberg, and also to the city of Berlin and even beyond. The building became an icon with which the wave of environmental design swept from London to Germany. This was shortly after reunification, a time when Germany was on the move – as was especially being manifested in Berlin. In the middle of this awakening, the GSW high-rise brought an important impulse and was an eye-opener for us – it felt like someone had just turned on a light.

The use of natural ventilation in a high-rise building, a double façade used as a solar chimney, the colourful design of a shading device – something that until GSW had been considered banal – and a passive system that was supplemented by innovative technology (coincidentally, using a technology that I had studied in my diploma thesis at just about the same time): suddenly, we could see that it was possible to materialise all of these innovative ideas in a large urban office structure – even in "stony" Berlin. We did not even know each other at the time, but the GSW building was nevertheless an important reference that ultimately also became a significant foundation for our own work.

## KfW Westarkade, Frankfurt

The KfW Westarkade was the initial project in my first collaboration with Sauerbruch Hutton almost twenty years ago. In this case, we were commissioned directly by the client – the German "KfW" Development Bank – and Sauerbruch Hutton won the design competition independently. It was, and still is, quite unusual for us to be commissioned by a client independently of the architects, and we had some concerns that these famous architects would not be very open-minded, especially since their design for the building was already quite developed. But to our surprise, the opposite turned out to be the case – they had no hesitation in rethinking everything. There was this continuous curiosity, which was one of the core principles that guided the entire design process. Right away, we understood that for them, "architecture today is not about a heroic individual … more than ever it is a team effort," as Matthias later said in a conversation. At that time, we had regarded the team as rock stars – and we still do – but we also got to know the "band". We learned that Louisa and Matthias, of course, have a special role in the office as frontwoman and frontman, but this never overbears the work on a project, as the design process is a true group effort that includes the entire team. It has always been a collaboration with respect and at eye level. The same was and is true of the architects themselves: Juan Lucas Young and Tom Geister were running the project and I never got the impression of a hierarchical interference within the office.

The KfW bank had high aspirations in terms of sustainability, which at that time basically meant minimising the use of energy in the operation of a building. This was a period when we – coming from the recent Stuttgart design tradition – tended to resolve this challenge with glass buildings that featured adaptable or smart façades. In this particular case, though, we recognised that the high-rise floor plate was not only formed like the wing of an aircraft, but that it was orientated perfectly, that is to say, straight into the direction of the prevailing wind. Together, we developed a sophisticated double façade system that used the wind to enable natural ventilation (at least in the shoulder seasons). This simple idea did, however, add a layer of considerable complexity, as the bank also requested a full mechanical

103

system for the extreme weather periods that occur during the summer and winter seasons. We ended up with an adaptive façade and a complex control regime. Unfortunately, we still do not really know just how well the building works (in energy terms). At times, however, one has an uneasy suspicion that its potential has yet to be fully tested – almost like an SUV that's used only to take the kids to school.

The architects used the regular vertical façade flaps, which function like a fish's gills, to apply their polychromy. It is an example of how such otherwise banal openings needed for natural ventilation can be used to define the particular beauty and architectural personality of a building. In terms of sustainability, though, we all had the impression that this project probably brought the idea of adaptability and complexity to a climax. After that, simplicity became the new keyword.

## State Ministry for Urban Development and the Environment, Hamburg

Right after the KfW building, Sauerbruch Hutton won the competition for Hamburg's State Ministry for Urban Development and the Environment, which became the flagship of the International Building Exhibition (IBA) in 2013. Such a public building, of course, had a budget that was considerably lower than that of a bank – a racing boat that features both engine and sails was clearly not an option. To stay within budget without compromising architectural quality, the architects decided to minimise the complexity of the mechanical systems. All the offices are naturally ventilated and have only minimal mechanical backup. The fenestration ratio is much lower than that of the KfW building. With their unshaded clerestory, however, the tall windows provide good daylight conditions. As a result of the reduced amount of glazing, the presence of external shading and the possibility to expose thermal mass (ceilings), the building can be heated largely through geothermal heat pumps and needs no mechanical cooling. In this, the moderate climate conditions of Hamburg are certainly helpful.

Even though we do not have any monitoring results, we all have the gut feeling that this building is probably working very well. After all, there is not much that can fail. In addition, we also assume that those who work in the building are quite satisfied, for we know from various research projects that users generally prefer natural ventilation to mechanical cooling. There are no building management systems that overrule users' choices; they feel – and are – in command. The building became an exemplary driver towards simplicity, not only for Sauerbruch Hutton. Today, we call this approach to sustainability "robust" design.

## Munich Re, Munich

In 2009, Sauerbruch Hutton were commissioned to convert an early computer centre in Munich that had been originally designed for Siemens Nixdorf into an office building for an insurance company. The key question became whether it was worthwhile to retain the 1980s superstructure with all its geometrical and structural constraints. After looking into the embodied carbon of the existing concrete frame, the architects agreed with the client that they should preserve their building structure, as it could be adapted and extended relatively easily. With this approach, there came to the fore a new aspect of sustainability that had been a pillar of SH's work since the early 2000s: the consideration of material use with its related issues, such as carbon emissions, scarcity of raw materials, end-of-life scenarios, expected lifetime and all the rest.

Questions of embodied carbon and life-cycle analyses are important benchmarks for the sustainable design of buildings and were already well researched by the time I was a student in the late 1980s – but back then, they tended to be applied only to the operational aspects of buildings and were not much considered in terms of the embedded energy of construction. Subsequently, this aspect came to be included in the sustainability assessment tool of the DGNB (German Sustainable Building Council), which was founded in 2007. So although Sauerbruch Hutton did not invent this field of operation, they were among the few practices that incorporated the topic into their decision-making design process fairly early on, and it was from this time that their attitude towards sustainability gained a new dimension.

## Woodie, Hamburg

The next evolutionary step in their sustainability journey was "Woodie", a project for a student residence in Hamburg. Here, for the first time, they used a modular construction for a seven-storey, 13,000-square-metre timber structure. The extensive use of this renewable, zero-carbon material and the off-site fabrication methods added another layer to the life-cycle considerations that had begun with the Siemens Nixdorf building in Munich. Typical for Sauerbruch Hutton is the façade design, for which they also used only wood for the cladding, illustrating again their quest for an ecological aesthetic. Like all their buildings, Woodie is embedded in an overall concept that considers the urban as well as the social fabric of its site.

**105**

Being a climate engineer myself, I have concentrated in this short essay on how I have witnessed the history of sustainable design over the last thirty years, as exemplified in buildings by Sauerbruch Hutton. However, their work cannot be reduced to one specific aspect such as sustainability, just as we cannot pick out one colour from the polychromy of their façades.

Instead, I would describe the process of their design as an intellectual reflection that is synthesised into a final piece of architecture in such a way that all contributing aspects are, on being combined, elevated to a higher level. The Indian architect Rahul Mehrotra once spoke about the relevance of the context of the context, that is to say, a system of references beyond any particular physical surroundings. The continuous questioning of basic principles is what the works of Sauerbruch Hutton reflect – that is why their work has never been fashionable, and why it is constantly evolving.

Have Sauerbruch Hutton unlocked the aesthetics of sustainable architecture in the thirty years of their practice? Probably not, as this is a never-ending process! But together, we are convinced that climate change, limited resources, global warming and the social divide have to be the key reference points in shaping our built environment. This concern for a wider perspective is in their DNA, as is their belief in the quality of a team over the individual hero – a fact that recently led them to change their office structure when they invited a wide group of long-term collaborators to become partners.

Angelika Fitz

# The Care Turn
# in Architecture

"Never demolish, never remove – always add, transform and reuse." With
this statement, the French architecture firm Lacaton & Vassal sums up its
approach to architecture. And notes that every now and then, it is better
to do nothing, not to build at all. An unusual attitude in the architectural profession. Some might think that the practice is undermining the foundations
of its own business. Yet it is precisely this attitude that will be honoured with
the Pritzker Prize in 2021. This choice signals a change of course for the
most prestigious international architecture prize that was already heralded
in Europe by the EU's Mies Award: expanding the horizon to encompass
more than the iconic constructions that had defined the 1990s, most particularly in the cultural sector. With the spotlight now turned onto large
residential estates from the 1960s and '70s, there is a growing focus on an
architecture that has already experienced several waves of criticism and
is currently acutely threatened by demolition. The decision to give the 2017
EU Mies Award to XVW architectuur and NL Architects for their conversion of
a prefabricated building in Kleiburg transmitted a forceful message. Two
years later, I was part of the Mies Award jury and – as the discussion moved
towards the three redeveloped large-scale residential buildings in the Cité du
Grand Parc in Bordeaux by Lacaton & Vassal, Frédéric Druot and Christophe
Hutin – we briefly wondered whether we were repeating ourselves. However,
the architectural solutions, the social structure and the economic models
involved are very different: in the Netherlands, individuality, ownership and
interiors completed by residents; in Bordeaux, a qualitative revolution within
social housing. Nevertheless, I am convinced that the issues raised by
these projects will be on the agenda for some time to come. In addition

to responses to existing architecture, these issues include housing, land and climate change. Almost half of the projects that we shortlisted for the 2019 Mies Award, including the M9 project, an urban regeneration scheme by Sauerbruch Hutton in Mestre, address further development of existing architecture. In this, I am not concerned with celebrating major architectural prizes, which always have their own dynamics, but perhaps such awards serve as seismographs for a new attitude, or can at least foster public debate.

## Repairing the future

Climate change has long been heading towards a climate catastrophe. Scientists constantly deliver their computed evidence, while a succession of UN conferences formulates political goals to mitigate climate change, most recently in the 2015 Paris Agreement. Thanks to movements such as Fridays for Future, the discussion has now reached a broad audience and the building sector has also grown aware of an increased need for enlightenment; sustainability is no longer a niche topic in architecture. The construction industry has a huge footprint in terms of both resources and emissions. The way we build now will play a decisive part, for example, in determining whether Europe will be climate-neutral in 2050, as envisaged in the European Commission's Green Deal. But above all, we need to set significantly more ambitious goals, for otherwise we run the risk that man-made ecological disasters will make the planet uninhabitable, as anthropologist Anna Tsing diagnoses: "Rapid climate change; massive extinctions; ocean acidification; slow-decaying pollutants; freshwater contamination; critical mutations of the ecosystem: industrialisation has proved far more deadly to life on earth than its designers might ever have dreamed."[1] The planet is suffering from petro-capitalism's violent, lethal effects. While the term "Anthropocene" describes an era shaped by humankind's impact on Earth, it simultaneously obscures the "Capitalocene".[2] Destructive ways of doing business have driven the planet into this existential crisis.[3] Architecture and urbanism, dominated by capital-oriented interests, are entangled in both ecological and social crises. That was the bad news. But the good news is that architecture can also be part of the solution. Achieving this, however, calls for a new ethics in architecture, new forms of cooperation and a planetary perspective that cares for the survival of all our planet's inhabitants and species.

In 2017, urban researcher and cultural theorist Elke Krasny and I began to transfer approaches from Care Theory to architecture and planning. In the publication C*ritical Care. Architecture and Urbanism for a Broken Planet*[4] and the eponymous exhibition at the Architekturzentrum Wien,[5] we presented this approach in theoretical texts and through numerous case studies. In an age of catastrophic destruction, we view an ethics of care – the "care perspective" – as the most important attitude for architecture and urbanism. Restoring the future to good condition can be secured only with a long-term commitment to planetary care based on human and non-human livability. Modernity, especially modernism in architecture and urban planning, combined the promise of a better future with a tabula rasa stance that holds echoes of colonialism. Today, we live with the consequences of this promise of a better future and are confronted with Earth on the brink of collapse. We propose a new attitude that no longer sets out to reinvent the future, but rather to repair it. "Critical care in architecture and urbanism is a starting point for not giving up on the future entirely."[6]

## Critical care

The planet is in an ICU ward and needs "intensive care". What form might an attitude of care and repair take in architecture and urban development? How can a care perspective help to ensure that architecture is not only conceptualised and envisioned differently, but also produces different outcomes? Elke Krasny and I refer to pioneers of care theory from political science and philosophy of science, such as Joan Tronto or María Puig de la Bellacasa. In 1991, Tronto, together with Berenice Fisher, defined care in the following terms: "On the most general level, we suggest that caring be viewed as a species activity that includes everything we do to maintain, continue, and repair our 'world' so that we can live in it as well as possible. That world includes our bodies, our selves, and our environment, all of which we seek to interweave in a complex, life-sustaining web."[7] "Critical Care" urges architecture and urban planning to contribute to this life-sustaining web. Humans and other species, technologies, labour and production relations are closely interconnected and interdependent, as are land, water and energy. The publication accompanying the exhibition that we made illustrates this in twenty-one contemporary case studies from all over the world. The latter demonstrate that architecture and urban development are not obliged to submit to the dictates of capital and the exploitation of resources and labour. Each of the projects redefines the relationships between economy, ecology and labour. A diverse range of protagonists are involved in ensuring care: those who work with architects and planners include activists, lawyers, anthropologists and artists, as well as municipal administrations and companies. Caring is always concrete; specific local conditions form the starting point, whether for flood protection with traditional low-$CO_2$ building techniques in Pakistan and Bangladesh, an ecological community land trust in Puerto Rico, new concepts for public spaces in Vienna, London and Nairobi or in dealing with existing architecture. Over the next few years, finding ways to tackle the built fabric of post-war modernism, with its grey energy but also with its aspirations for society and its cultural memory, will be a particularly relevant theme for the whole of Europe.

Back in 1989, Sauerbruch Hutton were already fostering the preservation of post-war heritage with the Paternoster Square project in London, which at the time appeared a provocative scheme, while also implementing a strategy in this spirit in their GSW Headquarters project in Berlin from 1990 to 1999. This entailed refurbishing and extending a 1960s high-rise that by the early 1990s had become a much-maligned part of the cityscape. Visible far and wide, the energy-saving convection façade with its coloured, movable sunshades has now become an urban landmark. In 2005 furthermore, Sauerbruch Hutton's design for the Federal Environmental Agency in Dessau integrated disused industrial and railway facilities, while in 2014, the practice refurbished and adapted a 1980s office building in Munich. Very recently, a conversion of, and rooftop addition to, an East German-era prefab school in Berlin was added to this list, along with the adaptive reuse of a pair of sites belonging to the Post Office: a 1960s tower in Constance and a large-scale administrative complex from the '80s in Hamburg.

At this point, I would also like to take another look at the project by Lacaton & Vassal, Frédéric Druot and Christophe Hutin in Bordeaux and show how an attitude of caring interweaves the idea of repairing the spatial, ecological, economic and social fabric. In many places, large housing estates from the 1960s and '70s no longer promise a better future but have become problematic. They suffer from mono-functionality, outdated structural engineering and technology, and, on top of all that, a poor image. In the Grand Parc in Bordeaux, three apartment blocks from the 1960s were rescued from planned demolition and underwent a renovation in terms of energy use and structure through minimal interventions. As well as updating technical installations and circulation areas, the crucial sleight of hand was the addition of prefabricated winter gardens that could be rapidly assembled in front in the existing façade, which had been generously opened up. With a variety of spatial options for summer and winter, these form a climatic buffer and increase the available space in each flat. The residents were able to remain in their flats during the conversion and are pleased with the flexible extra space and new spatial configuration: "I used to live in a rabbit hutch, now I live in a house," commented a long-standing tenant.[8] All of this and reduced energy costs, while the rent remained constant, since the non-commercial developer has no need to make a profit and can depreciate the investments over a long period. The economic advantages of existing versus new buildings are not always as obvious as this, partly because of a dearth of $CO_2$ pricing. In many places, not enough attention is paid either to complex criteria, such as those involved in the life cycle of buildings that harbour the potential of grey energy, or to the significance of buildings within their particular historical and cultural contexts. Even if existing buildings are inadequate, for example as regards their technical or urban-planning shortcomings, a care perspective will seek out ways to conceive a different future with existing resources.

When it comes to housing, the advantages of residential developments that incorporate open spaces and spatial leeway for additional functions became clear during the Covid pandemic, if not before. Over and above housing policy directed to the common good, redeveloping existing building stock can make an important contribution to creating good housing for everyone. Since the 2008 financial crisis, land prices in many places have been more significant cost drivers than construction costs. Private capital is increasingly taking flight into lucrative real estate, land speculation and land consumption are booming, investment funds are taking the place of developers, and buy-to-let flats are creating anonymous streets. Even small savers with their private pension provision are becoming part of this dynamic, which is partly caused by the pension funds and ultimately pushes up rents. It is also vital to factor in the ecological consequences of the ever-increasing sealing of the ground in both urban and rural areas, such as an acceleration of climate change and risks for food security.[9] Politicians and society do not seem to have learnt much from the last global crisis more than ten years ago. There has been no shift in the legislative framework to foster a sustainable and socially equitable architectural culture. And now?

## Will architecture survive?

This text is actually about the survival of the planet and its inhabitants. However, architecture and urban planning will become irrelevant before the planet is completely destroyed if they have nothing to contribute. "We have to change the way we work. We have to change the profession or architecture will not survive," notes the Pakistani architect and zero-carbon revolutionary Yasmeen Lari.[10] Architects need to become care-takers, nurturing the life-sustaining network shared by humans and other species. That includes caring for resources, labour relations and production conditions alike. While our call to incorporate a care perspective into architecture and urban planning was initially received with astonishment – "You mean architects should become care workers?" – the Covid pandemic has revealed a new scenario. The image of care workers has improved rapidly, and the interdependence of ecological, economic and social issues has become clear in the light of increasingly visible fault lines within society. Debate in the world of architecture now seems ripe for a care turn.

Numerous festivals, symposia and calls for proposals – such as the current London Festival of Architecture (Care, 2021) or the Future Architecture Platform (Landscapes of Care, 2020/21) – engage with the topic of "care". In order for the care turn to succeed both in practice and conceptually, architects must seek new alliances with different sites of knowledge, with activists and the world of politics, with different clients and with different financing models, including economic models for architectural production that allow for often time-consuming "maintenance work" and new interfaces between what we commonly call a top-down and a bottom-up approach. The Haus der Statistik project in Berlin is an interesting example of an alliance between civil-society "city makers" (urban stakeholders), administration and policy-makers that aims to attain neighbourhood development directed towards the common good. In San Juan, Puerto Rico, close cooperation between grassroots organisations and the municipal administration, as well as with lawyers, urban planners and environmental engineers, made it possible to establish the world's first Favela Community Land Trust. This trust not only secures the rights of inhabitants in the informal settlement, but also oversees ecological rehabilitation of this prime inner-city location, and at the same time prevents land speculation in the longer term. If architects are to find a role within such constellations or even initiate them, a changed mindset in architectural training and a post-heroic attitude in architecture as a whole will be crucial, as adopted by Denise Scott Brown already in the 1960s, inter alia in the urban planning and activist struggle against the Crosstown Expressway in Philadelphia's South Side, in which the neighbourhoods with the lowest-income groups were to be destroyed by the car-oriented city. Scott Brown proclaimed an attitude of shared caring to counter modernism's tabula rasa thinking. This attitude should prove ill-fated for an architect, especially a female architect. "No architect is prepared to conceive I'm an architect. They say, I'm a preservationist, I'm a planner, I'm part of the women's movement, I run the office — anything they don't care about at all. Don't let anyone think I'm a designer. It's hopeless,"[11] Scott Brown notes with hindsight. It is common knowledge that she did not win the Pritzker Prize, neither in 1991, when it was awarded to Robert Venturi, nor later. Architects today should no longer (have to) fear this. The care turn has arrived in architectural history.

1   Anna Tsing, "Earth Stalked by Man", *The Cambridge Journal of Anthropology*, 34, no. 1 (Spring 2016): 2.

2   See Donna Haraway, "Anthropocene, Capitalocene, Plantationocene, Chthulucene: Making Kin", *Environmental Humanities*, vol. 6, 2015.

3   See McKenzie Wark, *Molecular Red: Theory for the Anthropocene* (London: Verso, 2015); Jason W. Moore, *Capitalism in the Web of Life: Ecology and the Accumulation of Capital* (London: Verso, 2015); Jason W. Moore, *Anthropocene or Capitalocene? Nature, History, and the Crisis of Capitalism* (Oakland: PM Press, 2016).

4   Angelika Fitz, Elke Krasny and Architekturzentrum Wien (eds.), *Critical Care. Architecture and Urbanism for a Broken Planet* (Cambridge, Mass.: MIT Press, 2019).

5   "Critical Care. Architecture for a Broken Planet", exhibition at Architekturzentrum Wien 2019, curated by Angelika Fitz and Elke Krasny, https://www.azw.at/en/event/critical-care-architektur-und-urbanismus-fuer-einen-planeten-in-der-krise/ (accessed 21 May 2021).

6   Angelika Fitz, Elke Krasny, Architekturzentrum Wien (eds.), *Critical Care. Architecture and Urbanism for a Broken Planet* (Cambridge, Mass.: MIT Press, 2019), p. 12.

7   Joan C. Tronto and Berenice Fisher, "Toward a Feminist Theory of Caring", in *Circles of Care: Work and Identity in Women's Lives*, ed. Emily K. Abel and Margaret K. Nelson (Albany: State University of New York Press, 1990), p. 40.

8   In a conversation between the author and residents during the Mies Award jury site visit to Bordeaux in April 2019.

9   See Karoline Mayer, Katharine Ritter, Angelika Fitz and Architekturzentrum Wien (eds.), *Boden für Alle* (Zurich: Park Books, 2019); and the exhibition *Boden für Alle / Land for Us All* at Architekturzentrum Wien, https://www.azw.at/en/event/boden-fuer-alle/ (accessed 21 May 2021).

10   Yasmeen Lari in a Zoom conversation with Angelika Fitz and Elke Krasny, 29 March 2021.

11   Jeremy Eric Tenembaum, *Downtown Denise Scott Brown*, ed. Angelika Fitz, Katharina Ritter and Architekturzentrum Wien (Zurich: Park Books, 2018), p. 35.

# Scylla and Charybdis

Depending on whom you talk to, the thirty years since Sauerbruch Hutton started up their practice have either been very good for architecture, or very bad for it. Two developments in particular within the economic climate for new buildings have brought about these divergent accounts of contemporary architecture.

First of all, the freedom and speed with which buildings now circulate as images has led to the discovery of a new kind of value generated by buildings, a value unconnected to their traditional economic capacity to change land use and enhance rental value. Images of buildings now circulate so widely that even by themselves, those images have the power to bring benefits to the institutions, corporations or individuals who own the buildings, to the cities in which they stand and to the architects who designed them, regardless of the practical usefulness of the buildings themselves. In this way, buildings can act as "bait", bringing further investment to a locality and maybe rejuvenating ailing economies, thus creating an additional gain less tangible than that offered by a building's service function, but one that may far exceed the profits deriving from its practical use. This kind of value is not entirely new – to a very limited extent, a few buildings in previous times behaved similarly: cathedrals in medieval cities, St Peter's in Rome, the Eiffel Tower in Paris, and various other isolated monuments. But the accelerated circulation of images has brought about an explosion both in the magnitude of the effect and in the range of buildings capable of generating it: today, any building with a sufficiently strong image can become an attractor of this kind of value. What is sometimes described as the "Bilbao effect" – after Frank Gehry's Guggenheim Museum in Bilbao, which opened in 1997 – has proliferated beyond a few isolated examples and is no longer confined to cultural buildings. We now have mini-Bilbaos all over the place, as building owners everywhere aspire to capitalise upon this newly recognised potential.

Architects have been beneficiaries in this development, to the extent that the process places a premium upon uniqueness. The successful image will be that of a building like no other – and in realising this, architects, who have expertise in the production of the novel and the original, are well placed. In these new circumstances, it has become the task of architects "to provide unique and memorable experiences" – to quote the Brazilian architectural theorist Pedro Fiori Arantes, who has written perceptively about the whole phenomenon in his book *The Rent of Form* (2019). What is required of the architect is to provide such an experience, and in a form that can be mediated through an image. This expectation is very different from the modern era when, earlier in the 20th century, architects were encouraged to produce universal typologies, buildings that might become a standard capable of being replicated anywhere. The skills that went into that kind of work no longer apply in the new situation, where uniqueness is at a premium. To a certain degree, this change mirrors the one that has taken place within capitalism itself, where the greatest profits no longer accrue in quantities of goods manufactured, as was the case in the era of mass production, but come rather from the capacity to create or enhance meaning, where products acquire a status beyond that of being mere things. It is this shift, towards less emphasis on product innovation and more on the creation of aura around products, that marks the most profitable companies, and the shift is similar in relation to buildings – with the important difference that buildings remain tied to the ground in the places where they are built, and can never achieve the insubstantiality aspired to in the world of goods.

For architects, the demand for uniqueness has brought advantages, and has required them to concentrate upon certain aspects of buildings. In particular, attention to the external surfaces of buildings has become relatively more important than it used to be. Previously, architects operated with a relatively limited range of surface finishes. Now, a proportionately greater amount of an architect's ingenuity goes into devising novel surface effects, often so that the mass of the building is made to seem to dissolve beneath the image projected by the surface. To "reach the immaterial", in the words of Jacques Herzog, has become a frequent architectural aspiration. That architects find themselves obliged to commit so much of their creative effort to the design of surfaces is not entirely of their own choosing. Whereas once it was the disposition of interior spaces, the relations between users and occupied space – expressed through concepts such as "fit" and "flexibility" – and the relationship of buildings to their surroundings that absorbed most of an architect's attention, nowadays, whether they like it or not, architects find themselves expected to come up with novel and unique solutions to the external skin of buildings, because that is what will dominate the mediated image.

Some architects, especially those in design-led practices that specialise in the creation of singular buildings, have taken advantage of this situation and benefited from it. In a very few cases, they have achieved global fame and success, to an extent unimaginable to even the most famous architects in previous times. However, the temptation to pursue this market for singular buildings, advantageous though it has been, does come into conflict with other responsibilities to which architects pay recognition. If we take Rem Koolhaas' 2005 definition of an architect as "someone working for the public good" (was he being sincere, or ironical?), the attention to singularity is cast into sharp relief by the other major development of the last thirty years, namely the impact on building production of the neoliberal economic policies pursued in many Western countries.

The systematic and progressive deregulation of the construction industry and of urban planning, the cutting of "red tape" and of many regulatory procedures in the interest of speeding up construction and of enabling market forces to determine what happens, when and where, has certainly provided greater freedom in the creation of new buildings. On the one hand, these changes have offered architects increased scope to experiment with new designs and untried forms of construction. While certain regulations, especially those relating to energy use and $CO_2$ emissions, have become more stringent (thanks in part to the initiatives of architects and engineers), in other respects, such as standards for dwelling sizes, safety procedures and materials licencing, oversight has been reduced. Just as with the new value form of contemporary building, architects have been not only beneficiaries of the process of deregulation, but also its victims. In the interest of "risk management", we have seen a process by which responsibilities for safety, for quality assurances, are distributed along an ever-growing chain of agents, subcontractors and the like. As the ongoing public enquiry in the UK into the 2017 Grenfell Tower Fire disaster has shown, it becomes increasingly difficult to lay blame on any particular actor within the construction industry when something goes wrong, if no party is required to take ultimate authority for construction standards, whether for the quality of the building as a whole, or for any individual component of it. The culture of cost-cutting, buck-passing, risk avoidance has become unavoidable, indeed necessary, in modern-day construction. In this, architects are as complicit as anyone else, however much they might wish to take a stand against some of the practices of less scrupulous parties. Traditionally, architects were expected to protect the interests of clients, of builders, and of society at large. How well architects reconcile these divided, sometimes conflicting responsibilities is a mark of their ability. In the current situation, though, never has the opportunity for architects to act as the conscience of the construction sector as a whole been greater, even though their power to act is more circumscribed and diminished than ever.

How architects are to negotiate between the fresh opportunities presented by the new value form of buildings on the one hand, and the bear pit of a partially deregulated construction industry on the other hand, is a question that any architect entering practice in the last thirty years has had to confront. For those, like Sauerbruch Hutton, who have successfully navigated between the two without unduly compromising themselves, one can have only the greatest respect.

113

# 114

Philip Ursprung

# Images on the Move

By framing their own work between 1990 and 2020 with the surprising notion of the "turn of the century", Sauerbruch Hutton point at a challenge of architectural critique, namely the question of when a building moves from being a contemporary phenomenon to a historical one. The mere mention of "turn of the century" reminds one how uncertain the current concepts of time and of history are. It is difficult to draw the line between the contemporary and the historical in a situation where temporal succession is replaced by spatial juxtaposition, where the impression of simultaneity prevails and where the idea of progress gives way to the impression of stagnation. Notions that shape the image of European culture around 1900 – such as fin de siècle or avant-garde – are lacking for the phase around 2000. The once so prevalent buzzword "millennium" is now almost forgotten. Today, history does not resemble a book, where the turning of pages corresponds to the turn of centuries. Rather, history seems to unfold like a map where the past and the future blur into the impression of an omnipresent here and now.

When I moved to West Berlin in September 1989, East Berlin was virtually non-existent. Seen from the West, the other half of the city could be experienced only from underground. The subway maps indicated several stations located in the East as "stations where the trains do not stop". I remember ghost stations such as Alexanderplatz that were momentarily lit by the subway cars rushing through them. For some seconds, I could perceive a few benches and trash cans still standing on the empty platforms as if the passengers waiting for the subway had just left. These time capsules triggered my imagination and I imagined what the city was like before the separation, in 1961.

After the Berlin Wall opened in November 1989, I started to explore the East part of the city. The difference struck me, but it disappeared very rapidly. The socialist spatiality was literally absorbed, so to speak, by the capitalist spatiality. And this changed the entire city. The ruptures and anachronisms that had made Berlin so different from any other European metropolis were morphed in order to fit into the "smooth world" of globalisation, to para-phrase the definition given by Michael Hardt and Antonio Negri in their book *Empire*.[1] Soon, it became impossible to see where the Wall had once stood. Public monuments were demolished, street names changed, open spaces were reduced and streets became narrower. On the other hand, the nostalgia of a pre-modern past began to prevail in the guise of the "critical reconstruc-tion" of Berlin. The neoliberal city planners repressed the historical traces of the 20th century's tragedies and complexities with a mixture of nostalgic clichés and maximum flexibility for investors. The city centre turned into a theme park of 19th-century Berlin, culminating in the destruction of the socialist Palast der Republik and the project to replace it with a replica of the Baroque castle of the Prussian monarchy.

Disappointed by so many mediocre projects and missed opportunities, I was struck by the beauty of Sauerbruch Hutton's GSW Headquarters (1999). Suddenly, a building articulated the spatial and temporal specificity of Berlin. It worked like an instrument, like a powerful lens that allowed one to focus both on the East and the West, the past and the present. Located near the famous Checkpoint Charlie, GSW Headquarters mediates between the high-rise of the Axel Springer Verlag in the West and the *Plattenbauten*, prefab-ricated concrete tower blocks, in the East. Springer, the powerful right-wing media house, had been, for the generation of 1968, the very emblem of the reactionary attitude of Cold War Germany. Sauerbruch Hutton's colourful and dynamic building makes this somber version of the International Style appear even more rigid and overcome. And yet it treats it neighbour with respect. Its gesture towards the Springer building is not one of patricide or radical negation. Its relaxed curves, the playful rhythm of light and shadow, the transparency, the decorative colour scheme evoke another side of the 1950s, namely its vivid popular culture, playfulness, optimism, social mobility, and openness.

On the other hand, the GSW Headquarters acknowledges the existence of the high-rise buildings in the East. What is generally dismissed as an ugly symptom of scarcity, appears, in the light of Sauerbruch Hutton's building, as carefully placed elements of the skyline. It makes us perceive that socialist city planning did not reserve monumental scales for institutional architec-ture, but used it for housing the people. Sauerbruch Hutton help us under-stand that Berlin is a city where two spatial regimes meet. Long before the destruction of the Palace of the Republic was completed and the competi-tion for the Berlin castle replica was launched, they made a ground-breaking proposition for the future use of the site. Their proposal is a plea for the reminders of the past. In their words: "In a historic city, it seems natural to utilise these remains to the greatest possible extent and to activate them with various programmes." And they state: "The Palace of the Republic will be retained."[2]

Unlike most Western architects of an earlier generation, they have much sympathy for the East and a particular sensibility for what has been crushed by the political and economic change. East Germany, of course, is full of such traces of struggles. And in fact, the GSW Headquarters stands at the beginning of a series of their most interesting projects, all on the territory of the former German Democratic Republic, such as the Experimental Factory, Magdeburg (2001), the Town Hall, Hennigsdorf (2003), the Federal Environmental Agency, Dessau (2005) and, lately, two projects at Alexanderplatz, the very centre of the capital of the German Democratic Republic.

## Iconic turn

Much has been written on the technology and form of the GSW Headquarters. But how does it affect our perception? How does it achieve the particular effect of being a lens, making one see its context? The notion of the image and the discussion of the so-called iconic turn are helpful in following these questions. The trend towards the visual in most contemporary societies has been defined, in the 1990s, as "iconic turn" or, as it is sometimes called, "visual turn". Broadly speaking, the notion of the iconic turn refers to phenomena predominantly being perceived as images – in contrast to the earlier "linguistic turn", when phenomena were primarily received as texts and "read" as such. Whereas the iconic turn has triggered a vivid theoretical debate in various academic fields – the notion of the image being the common denominator between science, humanities and art – it has hardly affected the field of architecture. Like related notions such as "surface", "illusion", "theatricality" and "effect", the notion of image still holds a negative connotation among most architects. This doubtless has something to do with the fact that they think of the image as a picture – in other words, as a two-dimensional, framed object that is antithetical to the three-dimensional nature of architecture. The notion of image harks back to a latent, repressed fear that the autonomy of architecture is at risk as soon as architects draw too heavily on sources outside their own field. Furthermore, the discussion of iconic architecture – that is to say, of buildings that resemble works of art and can be perceived like paintings or sculptures – is limited because it reduces the complexity of architecture to analogies with the visual arts. But the concept of image has the potential to sharpen our understanding of contemporary architecture.

It is useful to go back to Henri Bergson's understanding of the notion of the image in his book *Matter and Memory*, first published in French in 1896, where he writes: "Matter, in our view, is an aggregate of 'images.' And by 'image' we mean a certain existence which is more than that which the idealist calls a *representation*, but less than that which the realist calls a *thing* – an existence placed halfway between the 'thing' and the 'representation'."[3] Bergson does not reduce the image to the notion of the flat, tangible painting, nor to its meaning as a symbol. In his view, images are not isolated, but are ever moving and permanently interacting, because we are always "in the presence of images, in the vaguest sense of the word, images perceived when my senses are opened to them, unperceived when they are closed. All these images act and react upon one another in all their elementary parts according to constant laws which I call laws of nature."[4] Jean-Paul Sartre goes even further when he declares that the image exists as "an act as much as a thing".[5]

The notion of the image as a dynamic tool that does something rather than as a passive representation is helpful for the current discussion of architecture. It allows us, for example, to compare the work of architects such as Sauerbruch Hutton, Herzog & de Meuron, Peter Zumthor, Rem Koolhaas, Caruso St John, Toyo Ito and many others. It also allows us to analyse different kinds of iconicity and distinguish landmark projects in the sense of drop sculptures such as Frank Gehry's Guggenheim Museum in Bilbao or Norman Foster's Swiss Re building in London, site-specific iconicity such as Herzog & de Meuron's Ricola Storage Building in Laufen, Switzerland, and the mere illustrative nature of, say, the replica of the Berlin castle. The GSW Headquarters plays an important role in this context because it combines different iconic levels. On the one hand, it attracts the viewer's gaze and provides orientation and pleasure for passers-by and the people who work inside. On the other hand, it absorbs the flow of spatial, temporal and mental images that saturate the city of Berlin. It not only refers to itself but transforms and articulates these images and makes us see its surroundings clearer.

## Images of labour

Among the buildings by Sauerbruch Hutton, none qualifies so precisely as "turn of the century" as the Experimental Factory in Magdeburg, designed and built between 1998 and 2001. But not only the numbers fit perfectly. It also resonates with three historical changes that mark the time between the late 1990s and early 2000s in Europe: German reunification after the peaceful revolution of 1989, the boom of higher education in the wake of the Bologna Process, and the transformation of human labour by digitalisation. The Experimental Factory is intrinsically linked to the dynamics of reunification in the 1990s and the massive growth of higher education and research in the wake of the European Research Area. Eager to catch up with the West half, the newly founded *Länder* in the former German Democratic Republic invested strongly during the 1990s in new university buildings, start-ups and research facilities. For a short period, the cards in the public sector were reshuffled. There was not only need for space, but also appetite for novelty. Never before or after this period were authorities so open to architectural experimentation. It is hard to imagine a project with the boldness of the Experimental Factory being carried out on a West German university campus around this time. The same goes for the two other prominent building realised for universities during the same period, both by Herzog & de Meuron: the Eberswalde Technical School Library (1999) and the Information, Communication and Media Centre (2004) at the Brandenburg University of Technology, in Cottbus.

Like the GSW Headquarters, the Experimental Factory strikes the visitors by its attraction. Again, it is located at an urban threshold, namely the area where the city centre of Magdeburg and the campus of the university and other research institutions meet. Nicknamed "silicon valley of Magdeburg" by its tenants, it houses various research facilities, either privately run or subsidised by the university. These functions are unified under what the architects call a large "blanket" in orange, pink and silver stripes. What I find particularly interesting is the fact that this blanket eludes the traditional concept of roof, or façade. It can be defined as a topological space where the distinction between inside and outside, up and down, roof and walls is blurred. Its complexity resists any overall view. From every angle, a different image can be perceived. It thus offers an alternative to the cliché of transparency and simplicity generally associated with factory constructions. Most people perceive it in movement, from their car, passing by on a busy, four-lane road. But it is also the only building in Magdeburg, as the plant manager proudly told me during my visit, that can be identified from the air by passengers flying to Berlin. The aerial view makes clear what one can only guess from the ground: that its shape makes the building look as if was cut out from a seemingly endless surface.

Like the GSW Headquarters, the Experimental Factory combines various iconic functions as a landmark building for the campus and the city. Its fresh colours – to me, they recall the flower power colours of the 1970s – stand in stark contrast to the shrinking city of Magdeburg, with its abandoned factories, ruined houses and a centre that is a palimpsest of Roman churches, Stalinist monumentality, 1970s *Plattenbauten* and 1990s shopping malls. It symbolises a new beginning and simultaneously refers to the student housing nearby, and to a steel bridge in the immediate neighbourhood. It also operates in the realm of the *musée imaginaire* of architecture. In the midst of deindustrialisation, it opens a dialogue with icons of industrial architecture, such as Peter Behrens' AEG Turbine Factory in Berlin (1910) and the Hat Factory in Luckenwalde by Erich Mendelsohn (1923), Ulrich Müther's nearby Hyperschale, in the centre of Magdeburg (1969), Ludwig Leo's Umlauftank 2 for the Versuchsanstalt für Wasserbau und Schiffbau in Berlin (1975) and Peter Eisenman's Greater Columbus Convention Center in Ohio (1993), a crucial project in the history of topological architecture.[6]

The imaginary conversation between the Experimental Factory and those buildings differs from the eclectic approach by architects such as Aldo Rossi or James Stirling. While such projects in Berlin as Stirling's Wissenschaftszentrum (1988) or Rossi's area of Schützenstraße (1997) incorporate historical typologies and fragments – and thus adhere to a historicist conception of time – the Experimental Factory is characteristic for an alternative temporal realm. Yes, it communicates with buildings of the past, such as expressionist factories, but as if these were all contemporary projects. Like an actor in a play that spans a century, it is open for exchange and interaction.

But the Factory does more than address the broad public and the experts. It is mainly a homage to the people working inside – and thus another gesture towards the culture of state socialism and its tradition of an iconography of work. The Factory functions like a stage where the act of research is framed and enhanced. The performative nature of the factory runs through the interior spaces. With its pink, orange and green colour scheme, the central two-storey foyer resembles a theatre lobby more than the entrance to a mere laboratory. And the main test hall can be overlooked from a gallery that connects the different parts of the building. When did one last see such spaces? They recall the expressionist spatiality of Erich Mendelsohn and the legendary workers' clubs by Konstantin Melnikov, and thus adhere to a tradition of architecture for workers, and an iconography of labour that has all but disappeared.

## Centre and periphery

With the Experimental Factory, Sauerbruch Hutton have proved that iconic architecture is not reserved only for cultural or corporate programmes. And they show us that urbanity does not take place only in the city centre, but at the outskirts, on the *terrain vague*, the wasteland, in areas not yet defined. Iconic architecture has the potential not only to activate such areas, but to articulate their specificity. The Sedus High-Bay Warehouse in Dogern (2003) is another example of the potential of iconicity. Although located in the idyllic context of the Black Forest landscape, it makes clear that the modernist dichotomy of landscape and the urban has collapsed and that there is nothing in our contemporary societies that is not urban. Whereas the GSW Headquarters mediates between images of capitalist and socialist space, the warehouse mediates between images of industry and "nature". The façade is covered by a coloured cladding system. As if some late 19th-century pointillist painting has merged with a gigantic computer screen, the image echoes the long tradition of landscape painting without restoring any idea of an untouched nature. Rather than claiming any harmony between industry and nature, Sauerbruch Hutton articulate the difference. Again, they are more interested in the collision between spatial regimes, in the analysis of the boundaries, than in a resolution.

Despite its location at the periphery, the warehouse is closely linked to another project: the Brandhorst Museum in Munich, which opened in early 2009. The colour cladding of the warehouse produces an effect of dematerialisation that makes the actual size of the building difficult to grasp. The same goes for the museum, clad in a combination of coloured ceramic battens and metal panels. Seen from nearby, the façade looks sculptural, tangible; seen from a distance, the elements blur into an overall atmospheric impression and produce a large array of beautiful effects. As in their earlier projects, Sauerbruch Hutton act and react simultaneously, mediating between spatial and temporal realms. Confronted with neighbours' protests against yet another large-scale cultural building, the architects designed a façade that partially absorbs the traffic noise. As if trying to withstand the massive presence of the nearby museum buildings – the Alte Pinakothek, the Neue Pinakothek and the Pinakothek der Moderne – its façade seems to dissolve, to evaporate. In the midst of an area densely packed with iconic buildings – to a degree that the images crystallise into clichés – the Brandhorst Museum makes the area move. Instead of presenting another image added to those of the existing museums, it brings into play a new kind of iconicity, one of vibration and constant change that affects its neighbours.

Be it the centre of the wealthiest city of Germany or a terrain in an area struck by poverty, Sauerbruch Hutton show us that centre and periphery, industrialisation and deindustrialisation, inside and outside, private and public are inseparably intertwined and constantly interacting. It is no coincidence that their architecture has, besides London, evolved mainly in Berlin, at the border between two economic, political and cultural regimes and during a phase of constant transformation. This conflict is articulated in the realm of images. Sauerbruch Hutton play a central role among those who have opened this space for architecture. Their iconicity makes us see what we know in theory but rarely perceive in our built environment, that there is no outside, no distance and no certainty. And they make us see that architecture, and we ourselves, can partake in changing this environment.

**119**

1   Michael Hardt and Antonio Negri, *Empire* (Cambridge, Mass.: Harvard University Press, 2000), p. xiii.

2   Sauerbruch Hutton, "Schlossplatz, Berlin, 2001", in *Sauerbruch Hutton. Archive* (Baden: Lars Müller Publishers, 2006), pp. 172–73, here: p. 172.

3   Henri Bergson, *Matter and Memory*, trans. N. M. Paul and W. S. Palmer (New York: Zone Books, 1991), p. 9

4   Ibid., p. 17.

5   Jean-Paul Sartre, *The Imaginary: A Phenomenological Psychology of the Imagination*, trans. Jonathan Webber (London and New York: Routledge, 2004), p. 20.

6   See Philip Ursprung, "Verwerfungslinien der globalisierten Welt: Peter Eisenman's Greater Columbus Convention Center (1993)", in Wolfram Pichler and Ralph Ubl (eds.), *Topologie, Falten, Knoten, Netze; Stülpungen in Kunst und Theorie* (Vienna: Turia + Kant, 2009), pp. 405–26.

120 Ola Kolehmainen

# Fluctuating Territories

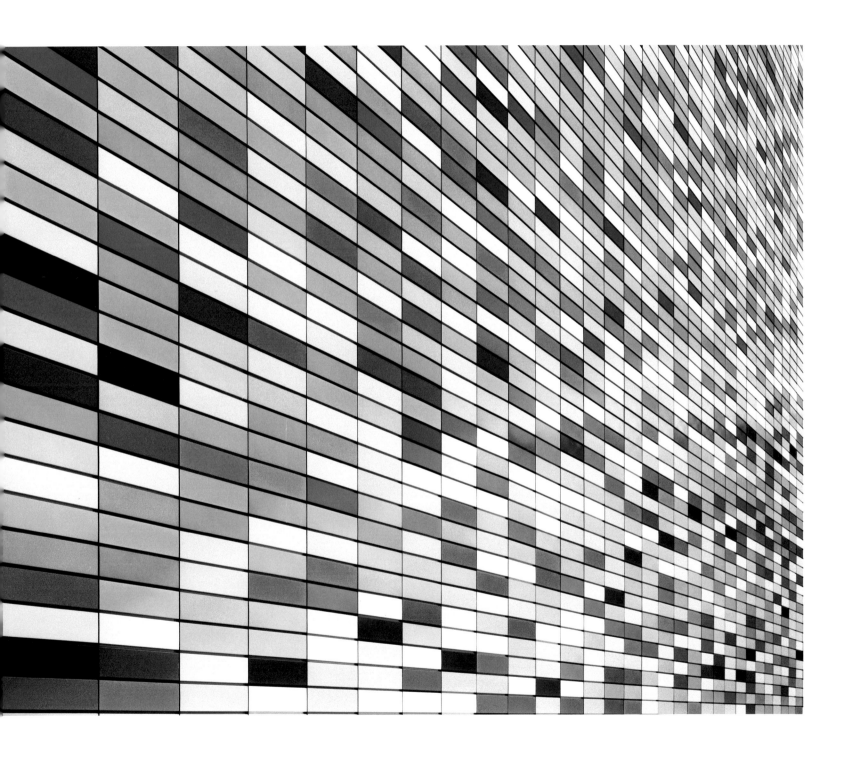

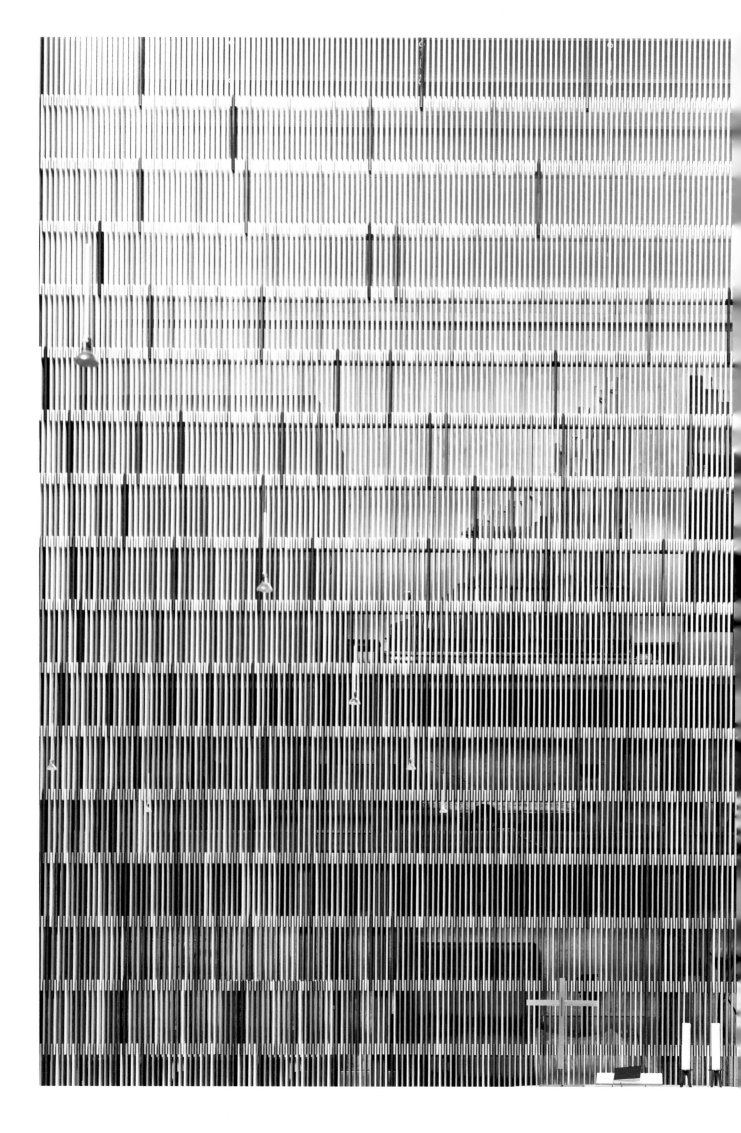

137

# 138

Gerhard Matzig

# Colour and Form

White can be the colour of purity. Sometimes, it is also the colour of longing. As I write this text about the rich wealth of colour in Sauerbruch Hutton's architecture, which, incidentally, is also impeccable in terms of form, it is snowing outside my window in Munich. At this very moment, the world is magically transformed – also suddenly transporting us, by association, into a snowstorm: the one that Hans Castorp experienced in Thomas Mann's *The Magic Mountain*.

In Mann's conception of art, which underlies this passage, art in particular transposes reality's bipolar nature from the commonplace, over-simplified concept of "either / or" into the genuinely true "both / and" of existence. The snow-covered landscape of that famous scene, swathed in hazy white, illustrates the realm of literary possibilities as a metaphor for variegated, divergent concepts of life. Mann describes this *coincidentia oppositorum* as the "artistic paradox". That brings us to colour in Sauerbruch Hutton's oeuvre, which proves virtually impossible to explain without addressing the non-colour white and its particular resonance in architectural history. How apt that it is snowing right now.

The amelanchier tree in the garden here has its moment as a sinuous arboreal sculpture full of voluptuous contrasts, silhouetted in dusky black against an ephemeral white landscape. That landscape becomes a canvas of the imagination. The falling snowflakes likewise unfurl an uncanny magic over the bleak drabness of an abysmally overcluttered suburbanity that is bloated with heterogeneous colours and forms. It is the magic of a uniquely colourless colour: white. Should I mention that, to boot, the house I am in is black? Two "non-colours", black on white, thus shape the inception of a text that nevertheless seeks to delve into the intensive use of colour in architecture created by Louisa Hutton and Matthias Sauerbruch. Perhaps that oddity is really not so odd after all. For this studio's powerfully evocative architecture incorporates the simultaneous existence of opposites that come together to form a harmonious whole.

Winter 2020 / 2021, stripped of sensory stimuli by the pandemic and with an apparently ever-more-pallid colour palette, nonetheless mercifully grants us the miracle of falling snow. That has become a rarity in Munich as it is elsewhere, and given that my roots lie in higher altitudes, I am immediately emotionally transported back to the deep, snow-covered forests and landscapes of my childhood. Like smell, colour is also always a space of memory and a resonance chamber. Marcel Proust's famous madeleine could theoretically be associated with a colour instead of with lime blossom tea.

So snow it is: what an almost exotic delight nowadays! – as imperilled by climate change as the polar bears' habitat in Greenland. It also proves to be a release for an author who has been staring for days now at the depressingly white surface of a "Word" document that keeps its distance as we all do these days, as unadulterated as it is blank and cold, simulating the whiteness of paper by analogy. White is also the colour of aloofness and emptiness.

And then, all at once, the idea – starting a text intended to celebrate colour with a homage to white, an achromatic additive non-colour – literally falls from the paradoxical heavens. Entirely palpable and crystal clear. As rational as the crystalline geometry of snowflakes. And paradoxically just as moving. Perhaps it is impossible to write about colours without bearing emotions in mind, too. Perhaps that is also a key to understanding Sauerbruch Hutton's architecture. For experiencing space is also always emotional rather than being purely rational. Colour in a work of architecture is therefore not only a variable in the formal and conceptual development of a design; it also enables the users to reclaim their sensuality as they appropriate a building.

That is precisely the aspect of their buildings that has long fascinated this critic: they can always be grasped spatially, quite literally. These are visceral, individual and powerful spaces, replete with character. Colour, however, is more than simply another dimension, for it is also the means that brings about the transformation: from seeing to feeling to grasping and permeating. Spaces in the sense understood by this studio are also always spaces of possibility within the universe of *The Magic Mountain*.

Nevertheless, white is not exactly the colour that first springs to mind when one thinks of Louisa Hutton and Matthias Sauerbruch's vibrant architecture, which, though it always makes vigorous use of colour, is anything but brightly coloured. And yet it makes sense to conceptualise this encounter with the colour-intensive world of form (which, we should not forget, is also a form-intensive world of colour) by thinking about a colour that, on the one hand, is not a colour at all, although physics teaches us that in the form of white light, it does contain all the colours of the visible spectrum. In a certain sense, white is the colour par excellence. Perhaps that is precisely why such heated debates have been ignited about this ostensibly cold colour in recent architectural history. Looking at the entire architectural reception of modernism, white can hardly leave you cold.

The Weißenhofsiedlung, for example – built in 1927 as a showcase for *Neues Bauen* (New Building) at the beginning of the 20th century (almost at the same time, incidentally, as *The Magic Mountain* was first published, in 1924) – was lambasted by the National Socialists as an "Arab village". That was not solely a reference to its predominantly cube-shaped architecture. It was also because the Weißenhofsiedlung's colour scheme in a sense reflects its name, which stems from the premises of baker Georg Philipp Weiß ("White"). Many of the emblematic experimental buildings, designed for example by Mart Stam, J.J.P. Oud, Hans Scharoun or Le Corbusier, deliberately opted to use white. This colour, which denotes a fresh start, is part of the architectural programme. The point was to overcome history, not merely for the sake of adopting an anti-historical pose – that would be too simplistic – but as a response to the social afflictions that led to the First World War. The "new" is held to offer a remedy. Distrust of the "old" does not arise simply because it is old, but because it appears corrupted at times.

The new human thus constitutes the goal for the new architecture. This stance was not so much presumptuous as full of yearning, as is still the case today. And it was, of course, also somewhat naive, as the history of the Second

World War demonstrates. However, acknowledging this motivation is essential in order to do justice to modernism, even if there is a lingering scepticism about some of its clean-sweep radicalism, especially in urban planning. As to the colour white: it nevertheless became a code signifying inner renewal for generations of architects. National Socialist propaganda preferred to talk about it as a façade colour that could hardly be more "un-German".

Photomontages with racist undertones soon appeared, mocking the Weißenhofsiedlung as home to carpet traders, camels and dates. A regime that associated itself with "earthy" brown (which was meant to symbolise the homeland and the soil) apparently had no use for white as a colour. White is, perhaps understandably, also the colour of innocence and purity, at least in terms of Western societal and cultural connotations. Incidentally, the history of architecture had the last laugh: first, the Bauhaus, like modernism as a whole, is anything but averse to colour – and second, the white that was supposedly the distinctive Bauhaus colour became famous internationally only because its protagonists had been exiled after the destruction of their art school. The Nazis, aiming for a Germanic architecture, seem to have inadvertently invented the International Style. Too bad for them!

National Socialist criticism of the colour preferred by the Bauhaus only for exteriors became so emblematic that in the resulting confusion, you could almost forget that modernism is about more than merely a dearth of colour – a reproach that is far from being a prerogative of barbarism. Criticism of a form of modernism that is perceived as colourless and cold, not to mention aloof and distant, is as old as modernism itself. Its manifestations range from Nazi tirades against white as something exotic to Ernst Bloch's dictum (buildings that seem "ready to go", rootless), not to mention Tom Wolfe's gleeful anti-Bauhaus invective against this type of modernism and the "whiteness & lightness & leanness & cleanness & bareness & spareness" that pervaded buildings tiled like glistening insecticide refineries, the way the colour white did. It is worth noting that Wolfe, an American man of letters who always sported a fine, impeccable but, above all, white suit, was most certainly fond of this colour – just not as an architectural code of classical modernism.

On a side note, the polemical verve of Wolfe's slim volume *From Bauhaus to Our House*, which caused such a stir among modernism sceptics against the backdrop of rampant post-modernism in the 1980s, also chimed with an advert for McDonald's, that renowned purveyor of hamburgers. The commercial depicts an architect showing a young couple around the new abode he has designed for them. Dressed in stereotypical black, he opens the door to the living room. The camera zooms in to reveal the typical glistening interior so beloved of glossy lifestyle magazines: white tiles on the walls, floor, and ceiling. Not a scrap of fabric. But above all, no colour anywhere. Tom Wolfe would have talked about being "driven to the edge of sensory deprivation". A moment later, the woman of the house plucks up her courage and asks: "But isn't it a bit cold?" With a sardonic grin, the architect responds: "If you want something warm, you'd better go to McDonald's." The punchline is reminiscent of the kind of elite-bashing that has become even more widespread nowadays. But it also reminds us that modernism sometimes does not have to be assessed quite as positively as its most stalwart advocates imagine.

While properties touted on real-estate portals as "Bauhaus" villas often prove to be somewhat misleading in their descriptions, for they are virtually indistinguishable from rough-hewn sugar cubes couched as family homes (in other words: they are neither villas nor have anything to do with the Bauhaus), white does at least still rule the roost in this context. That is somewhat strange, for it has actually fallen out of favour. Use of colour for interiors and exteriors already enjoyed a revival some years ago. Take a look around the suburbs – where the Swedish-style houses are painted red, those that yearn for Greece are blue, and what could be read as reminiscences of Tuscany are daubed in yellowish hues – and rejoice. At least if you want to misunderstand modernism in the McDonald's sense, even though from Gropius to Le Corbusier, it was often replete with colour (just as the temples of antiquity are white only in antiquitising classicist misconceptions).

That said, it has now become almost impossible to fend off this new chromatic onslaught, whether inside or out. These days, you would be quite justified in dreading it, for it often provides a painful demonstration of what distinguishes a deliberately, deftly coloured world from the random use of every possible shade of crayon. Louisa Hutton and Matthias Sauerbruch's deployment of colour in architecture teaches us something quite different from the garish hues of DIY stores: colour is an architectonic means that relies on knowledge, in the same way that architectonic form does, in order to come together and constitute architectural culture. Architectural practices that have worked with colour for many years – in other words, tapping into it as a traditional yet innovative driving force permeating all architectural styles – have not restored to houses and cities this facet that modernism (seemingly) denied them. They did not invent colour but rediscovered it, in Luigi Snozzi's sense. That merits recognition. This is one of the reasons why you sometimes find yourself standing in front of a building by Sauerbruch Hutton and revelling in the precision with which colour is deployed, as if you were bathing in the light. Which, by the way, is white, and all colours, too: architecture of colour is architecture of light.

White is wonderful. However, it becomes a problem when this beautiful achromatic colour is not understood spatially but only as a cipher. In other words, when it serves only to document the primacy of form. In that case, white becomes a canvas of emptiness. That is why form is no less germane than colour in Sauerbruch Hutton's architecture. Indeed, the approach adopted runs counter to any such idea of precedence: the colour does not dominate the form – it is all about coexistence and mutual authentication. In Mann's sense, rather than a haphazard "or-maybe-that-too" rhetoric, Sauerbruch Hutton's polychromatic architecture embodies a form of precise "both / and" architecture that is unconditionally just the way it is and sets as much store by colour as by form – and vice versa.

This architecture holds such riches because it dwells in spaces that are also always spaces grounded in colour. To quote Le Corbusier, architecture is "the masterly [...] play of volumes brought together under light". The light, however, is the colour white. And even more than that: all colours. Sauerbruch Hutton do not simply construct architecture that also happens to be very colourful. They write architectural history by reconciling material, light and space with colour, a dimension many believe to have been lost, while on the other hand, it is often unthinkingly resuscitated. The buildings that have emerged from this stance and continue to grow out of it are celebrations not of colour but of a consummate whole.

Kurt W. Forster

# Dammi i colori[1]

Recent decades have brought massive change in most sectors of life and no less in the domain of architecture. They range from the more obvious prêt-à-porter of post-modernism to the telluric manifestation of a practice based on algorithmic control.[2] In the life of a single generation, architecture and its production fashioned an entirely new basis. Closely observing these processes may exaggerate their magnitude, but looking back upon them suggests more than a mere "turn" to be followed by another. Isolating architecture from the larger picture of production and consumption highlights some peculiar aspects – such as the rapid adoption of computational tools throughout the building trades – but it also distorts the issue of design and its implications in the struggle with political and environmental realities. The return of colour and materials such as ceramics, no less than the insistent call for fresh air and calibrated light,[3] recyclable materials and an altogether different approach to building, were surely bound to affect more than the surface and the ephemeral feel of many structures. However late and slow, new values and their material implications mark a decisive transformation and reopen issues that had been considered shut.[4] On the one hand, colour directs attention back to the material components with which they originated and by which they affect the public, and on the other, to how subjective qualities fare under the conditions of a near-total digital regime. Whenever such issues emerge with suddenness and a certain urgency, it is worth exploring their deeper roots in order to recognise their family history rather than merely diagnose a childhood disease.

Among the many matters that occupied Gottfried Semper, once he had chosen architecture as his profession, colour held a special place, as it had done since his student days in Paris. It was also a topic that interested historians such as Quatremère de Quincy and architects such as Jacques-Ignace Hittorf. Semper's mentor, Karl Friedrich Schinkel, who recommended him for appointment in Dresden and whose exceptional career as a designer of stage sets drew heavily on colour and their emotional effects, refreshed Charlottenhof with the colours he had studied in Pompeii. Following in Schinkel's footsteps and extending them to Greek antiquities, Semper boldly reconstructed the appearance of the Athenian Acropolis with earthy colours. He pursued his quest for polychromy not only in opposition to a lingering dogma of the times, based on the purist convictions of Johann Joachim Winckelmann, but also as an extension of French interests he had known since his time as a student. The rich harvest of architectural evidence he personally gathered in Greece made Semper look for an opportunity to publish his findings in France. He even prepared covers in the fashion of Pompeiian wall paintings, and although he did not find any takers, the luminous plates he had prepared make a powerful impression even today, when colour has, on the whole, lost some of the impact it still enjoyed in the 1830s. Not all was lost, however, for Semper managed to produce his pamphlet *Vorläufige Bemerkungen über bemalte Architectur und Plastik bei den Alten* (Preliminary

Remarks on Polychrome Architecture and Sculpture in Antiquity) in 1834. This may have helped to secure his appointment to a professorship at the Academy of Fine Arts in Dresden, where, a few years later, he went on to emblazon the interior of his synagogue and, to ravishing success, his Opera House.[5]

It may be coincidental and yet indirectly significant that Semper explored Greece during a period of political turbulence, when the prospect of a young Bavarian prince becoming king of a newly constituted country triggered opposition and unleashed military insurrection. Travelling in the company of Friedrich Theodor Thiersch, a historian of antiquity and unofficial agent who negotiated with rebels, representatives of changing alliances, and local warlords, even fending off pirates, Semper took time to explore remote sites and document the traces of colour he found on carved marble. It is as if the violence and danger that beset Semper during his studies added a blush of excitement and purpled his view of what was, in any case, his personal quest for a fresh quality of architecture, unsuspected at the time but consequential thereafter.

Architectural polychromy was discovered in relatively remote places on the Peloponnese and in Sicily, but its survival in vernacular practice up to the present added to the recognition of its importance. The excavator of the temple at Bassae, Baron von Stackelberg, embedded what he found on the marbles of ancient Doric temples in a vision of a Mediterranean climate that continued to favour this practice and made "the Doric temple appear much more richly decorated than one can imagine".[6] He was not alone among travellers who wished to see in ancient temples and sculptures the achievements of a culture resplendent in its own materials and their shining qualities. In the eyes of archaeologist and architects, no less than in those of Friedrich Nietzsche and Semper, architecture had reclaimed its raiment of saturated earthen hues. Its festive appearance in Semper's and Hittorff's watercolours amounts to a wake-up call for polychromy, and the blazing tones of Semper's friend Richard Wagner chimed in with a fresh appetite for emotional intensity and fiery display.

As the power, quality and psychological effects of colours began to be recognised, including their effect on one another, different fields of study converged on this subject.[7] It was quickly discovered that some colours enhance luminosity and others dampen or suppress it, and that the entire spectrum of refraction would lead to a true understanding of their nature. No surprise, then, that experts as diverse as the horticulturist John Paxton and the architect, graphic artist and pioneering printer Owen Jones would join forces in designing the Crystal Palace for the Great Exhibition of 1851 in London. Using coloured glass and especially employing polychromy across all of the structural members of this fabulous canopy, Jones enabled Paxton to achieve the desired effect: "In the decoration of the Exhibition," Jones explained, "I propose to use the colours blue, red, and yellow, in such relative quantities as to neutralise or destroy each other." In his experiments in chromolithographic printing and with his knowledge of ornament, Jones drew on the theories of the French chemist Michel-Eugène Chevreul, the scientific mind behind the colouristic experiments of the Impressionist painters, and he credited "Mr. Field, in his admirable works on colour," because he "has shown by direct experiment that white light consists of blue, red, and yellow, neutralising each other in the proportions of eight, five, and three."[8] Jones' calibration of colours – derived from George Field's *Chromatography; or, a Treatise on Colours and Pigments, and of their Powers in Painting* (1835) –

in turn refined earlier efforts to diffract light and measure the relative quantity of its spectra.

Once brought to light, there was no stopping the use of resonant colour inside theatres, such as at Hittorff's Cirque d'Hiver in Paris, exquisitely painted by Edgar Degas, and in many public buildings and private villas. Their exteriors tended to stony reserve and inflated demeanour, but colour triumphed indoors, in velvet upholstery, damask and silk curtains, and wine-red carpets, before its chromatic register lightened and ignited the Jugendstil palette with emerald greens and yellows. Gold, silver and cobalt blue thread the edges of porcelain plates, the hems of trailing dresses and the stained glass of many a stairwell. Colour, in a word, was back, only to be flung onto the heap of history by the First World War.

The war not only silenced an often exuberant tenor of life, sinking the spectacle of the belle époque like the *Titanic*, it also drowned everything in mud and dust, leaving behind a bleak world in need of rebuilding. In such conditions, the effort to think of art as integral to a new future endowed the Bauhaus in Weimar with its signal role. The foundational curriculum treated colour the same way it did clay, wood, iron, glass and fibres – as the stuff of all artefacts – and the basis of its workshops as an extension of Semper's approach. Proclaiming a new social purpose for art, the Bauhaus led back to basics and, by the same token, aimed to transcend what still remained of the social order. It declared *Bauen* (building) to be the paramount collective achievement, which, although still out of reach, lit a beacon for all to follow. In the *Vorkurs*, the initiatory groundwork for all students, every subject was based on a material, among which colour and ceramics reclaimed their "elementary" share, recalling the craft practices that had established themselves across millennia.

It may astonish us that Gropius called several painters to the Bauhaus but no architects, and that the school was slow in approaching its ultimate goal, whereas a great deal of time went into initiatory exercises, with colour, drawing and painting holding centre stage.[9] Several courses hinged on the conjunction between colour, light, motion and sound. Ground-breaking lessons to be drawn from these explorations took shape in Paul Klee's and Josef Albers' studios. Both also provided a springboard for the nearly worldwide impact of the Bauhaus, with Albers' treatise on the *Interaction of Color*, first published in 1963, a late but especially powerful result.[10] Once again, the new proved to be a return, not a return to the recent past whose indulgencies and excesses landed on the scrapheap but to a more archaic past. The past that suddenly mattered was one of *beginnings*. And how better to begin afresh than by picking up the actual materials themselves? This did more than satisfy a desire for a down-to-earth approach; it also helped to build a bridge to manufacturing, to industry, and to a new sensibility for primary experiences. Clay emerged as a singularly appropriate material for learning to shape matter. Well beyond the fact that it was "dirt cheap" – compared with woods, metals and glass fit for refined workmanship – clay served as the primer for basic instruction at Vkhutemas, the Russian state art and technical school founded in Moscow in 1920,[11] and it had, of course, a millennial history in brick and tile. For good reason, the American architect Louis Sullivan had found in terracotta the very medium, even the embodiment, of his architectural aspirations. His erstwhile draughtsman Frank L. Wright recognised that "all materials were only one material to [Sullivan] in which to weave the stuff of his dreams".[12] In an advertising brochure for the Bayard Building in New York, Sullivan spoke of clay out of a somnambulist vision: "terracotta" he declared, "is older than civilization yet very new in its modern applications. [...] It does a great job protecting the steel-frame method from fire" and, he went on to explain, "it is the most plastic of materials in its raw state, suffering itself to be shaped, with marvelous readiness into ever conceivable delicacy and variety of form and movement, yet, when once fired, these forms and delicacies become everlasting."[13]

The terracotta-clad tall building was thus born of dual origin: as an utterly modern and a thoroughly ancient creature (with next to nothing in between). In addition to casting wonderfully tactile sheathing for his robust buildings, Sullivan also employed glazed terracotta, and with some of his late work produced fabulous polychromous work that fulfilled his wish for buildings with a "life of their own". The singular blend of ease in shaping and durability in the result destined glazed terracotta for yet another season. It is fair to say that some of Sauerbruch Hutton's most remarkable buildings began, step by step, to restore the potential of glazed terracotta to a place it rarely ever enjoyed in secular buildings.

Colour came first, followed by ceramics, and more and more ingenious applications of glazed terracotta. Beginning with the GSW Headquarters in Berlin (1991–99), where colour emblazoned the movable shades behind the gently curving curtain wall and low perimeter buildings assumed their identity through large-format anthracite tiles,[14] the Experimental Factory in Magdeburg (2000–01) extended bands of colour over the entire envelope of the structure. Among numerous other publications, it featured in a special volume produced by Tsinghua University as an early instance of "*Colour in Architecture*", sharing the pages with such buildings as the Santa Caterina Market in Barcelona, which threw a flying carpet of brilliantly coloured hexagonal tiles over a salvaged structure.[15] With the new millennium, glazed terracotta returned to architecture in a remarkable variety of ways, albeit mainly limited to buildings considered to be closely related to art – as if the archaic resonances and the intensity of visual presence were somehow shunned by more pedestrian projects, when it had in fact been a "vernacular practice" that had kept terracotta in use, however attenuated, for centuries.[16] Sauerbruch Hutton have taken the familiar qualities of glazed terracotta beyond the range of previous applications. For the Brandhorst Museum in Munich, they crafted glazed vertical staffs in a rich palette of hues that set the building's fine-grained surfaces into optical vibration. Rendering the museum's presence pictorial and eminently plastic at one and the same time, the interplay of colour and ceramics recovers the archaic duality of malleable matter and flickering light as the defining quality of a building. Colour, its material carrier and the conditions created by the buildings in their environment constitute a polyphonic whole rather than accretions of one another. Colours set the tone, material surfaces lend character, and the shapes of volumes and spaces orchestrate their vibrancy.

1   The artist Mario Cavaradossi asking for colours: "*Dammi i colori... Recondita armonia di bellezze diverse !*", in Giacomo Puccini's opera Tosca, libretto by Giuseppe Giacosa and Luigi Illica, first performed in Rome in 1900.

2   See Mario Carpo, *The Alphabet and the Algorithm* (Cambridge, Mass.: MIT Press, 2011) and *The Second Digital Turn* (Cambridge, Mass.: MIT Press, 2017). Carpo's studies, developed from his previous investigation of how the print media transformed architecture, go further than the analysis of technologies by recognising their constitutive role in contemporary culture.

3   Kurt W. Forster, "Light in Architecture", in *Light in Architecture and Art: The Work of Dan Flavin* (Marfa, Tex.: The Chinati Foundation, 2002), pp. 9–38.

4   Elena Manferdini and Christina Griggs, "Color Corrections", in *Log* 49 (Summer 2020): 105–09: "If architecture today must engage with the full color spectrum, then the question of what that might mean for our creative field is unavoidable."

5   Harry Francis Mallgrave, *Gottfried Semper, Architect of the Nineteenth Century* (New Haven & London: Yale University Press, 1996) gives a succinct account of Semper's travels and his often perilous exploration of ancient Greek temples, from the Acropolis to the Peloponnese, and of his study of Etruscan tombs and Pompeii, pp. 44–56.

6   O.M. von Stackelberg, *Die Apollotempel zu Bassae in Arcadien und die daselbst ausgegrabenen Bildwerke* (Rome, 1826), p. 33.

**146**

7   *Goethes Farbenlehre und die Lehren von den Farben und dem Färben* (catalogue, Petersberg: Imhof, 2010) offers a wide-ranging documentation of colour theory and its applications to the manufacture of dyes, including contributions by such little-recognised figures as Wilhelm Ostwald and Albert Heim.

8   Owen Jones in the official publication, *The Great Exhibition* (London, 1851), unpaginated.

9   Linn Burchert, Gertrud Grunow 1870–1944. L*eben, Werk und Wirken am Bauhaus und darüber hinaus*, e-book (Open Access), e-doc-Server der Humboldt-Universität zu Berlin, Nov. 2018, DOI: https://doi.org/10.18452/19512 (accessed 9 May 2021).

10   Paul Klee, *Pedagogical Sketchbook*, Walter Gropius and László Moholy-Nagy (eds.). Bauhaus Bücher (Weimar, 1924) and more extensive notes published posthumously as *Schriften zur Form und Gestaltungslehre*, ed. Jürg Spiller, (Zurich, 1956) and Josef Albers, *Interaction of Color* (New Haven and London: Yale University Press, 1963). It is worth noting that "colour" was also intermittently taught at the Bauhaus by Gertrud Grunow, a singer and dancer who gave classes in colour harmonisation, and by the chemist Wilhelm Ostwald, who created sets of standard colours based on the properties of inert matter.

11   See Anna Bokov, *Vkhutemas and the Pedagogy of Space*, 1920–1930 (Zurich: Park, 2020), where the frontispiece shows the studio exhibition of clay models, c. 1927..

12   Frank L. Wright, *The Natural House* (New York: Horizon, 1934), p. 24.

13   Quoted from William Jordy, "The Tall Buildings", in *Louis Sullivan, The Function of Ornament*, ed. Wim de Wit, (Chicago Historical Society, The Saint Louis Art Museum: 1986), p. 104.

14   A practice recalling black tiles on the ground-floor elevation of buildings by Otto R. Salvisberg in Berlin and Zurich, where he was professor of architecture from 1929 to 1940.

15   *World Architecture* [with Tsinghua University], 159 (September 2003), *Colour in Architecture* includes Sauerbruch and Hutton's Experimental Factory in Magdeburg, a curving envelope, described by the architects as a "blanket … draped over the undulating envelope" (p. 52) – sharing its moment with Miralles Tagliabue's Barcelona market. Several examples included in this issue of *World Architecture* also address materials by, and on, which colour is introduced, as well as exposure, lighting and the more elusive effects of reflection, gradation and fading.

16   *La Ruta de la Cerámica* (Castellón, 2000), catalogue of an exhibition documenting the use of ceramics from Mesopotamia and China to 19th-century Iberia.

# Collaboration

My work as an artist almost always involves developing and implementing my ideas in close collaboration with people who work in different professions, for example with programmers, engineers, architects, designers, and so on. This mostly happens in the context of very time-consuming processes, sometimes lasting years, in which we meet repeatedly, discuss details and learn from each other. When such collaboration runs smoothly, the encounter generally extends beyond merely a single joint project. That is what happened with Matthias Sauerbruch and Louisa Hutton. Over and above our appreciation for each other's work, we have been friends for many years now. This meant that we already had a solid shared foundation when it came to conceiving the spaces for my studio and living area.

Although I naturally intended to work in the studio and live in the residential part, right from the outset, I did not assume only the role of a commissioning client, as my artistic method also leads to solutions that merit discussion and are interesting for others, over and above my purely individual requirements. As far as I was concerned, this particular construction project turned into a vehicle for reflection upon the general conditions that underlie artistic work. My concept for combining studio and apartment, in such a way that every space has the potential to be either a working or a living area, springs quite naturally from my own artistic practice. At the same time, it also reacts to what are described as "post-studio practices", a term that highlights the fact that all kinds of media and techniques can be incorporated when making art. That is why, at first glance, artists' workplaces these days often resemble scientific laboratories or planning offices rather than one's conventional image of a painter's or sculptor's workshop.

As, unfortunately, I can never foresee which working processes will be required for forthcoming projects, I needed a place that would be "future-proof". This, in turn, presupposed thinking about spaces that would be as open and flexible as possible – for how could I possibly know now how I might want to live and work in ten years' time? It was not even entirely certain that I would still be working here at that point – I could also imagine inviting guests to these spaces or presenting exhibitions here or hosting cooking events or symposia! In any case, in commissioning this project, it was important for me to remain open to what other artists, even fictitious ones, might need and therefore to create spaces full of possibilities. The quest to achieve universal functionality meant that many iterations of the plans were needed, which, although at times annoying, usually led us to new insights.

Through our collaboration, we have succeeded in realising a project that incorporated the unpredictable as one of the planning parameters and that remained inspiring throughout the entire process, for both parties, I think. I remember one meeting in which some of the builders used six planks to simulate a wall, like a real-world model simulation, and carried them back

**148**

and forth to demonstrate, one after the other, how our various proposals would look. As an artist, I am not used to deciding on the basis of plans, but tend instead to use a 3D model, preferably on a 1:1 scale. In architecture, of course, such a full-scaled approach would rapidly trigger a logistical and financial disaster. However, working together, we came up with some wonderful solutions by being prepared to meet each other halfway in our respective working methods. This meant we collaborated in the truest sense of the term – that is to say, we were able to create a single piece of work together.

That is how, for example, we came up with the small, mirror-image twinned rooms that lie behind a special door-wall combination. Perhaps the idea of reflection that I have long pursued is a good symbol of our cooperation. Like the two hemispheres of the brain, this pair of rooms can also form a single room, yet at the same time, the two rooms are conceived as mirrored spaces of reflection that are identical. In a similar vein, I believe that my first work in and with the new studio, *Fenster DIN A4 / DIN A3* [Window A4 / A3],* also represents the intertwining of artistic and architectural thinking: the counter-perspectival expansion of the field of vision echoes the industrial standards for the two most widespread paper formats and thus establishes a practical and symbolical connection between the media that engage me: spaces, papers, perspectives.

The ensemble of studios and spaces developed in this way is a joint work that maintains the creative imprint of those involved. I can now say, some ten years later, that I still find it inspiring to live and work here.

*   *Fenster / Window DIN A4 < DIN A3, 2009, 42 × 36.5 × 29.7 cm* comprises an A3-sized window set flush within the studio's exterior wall, which is framelessly glazed. Sloping reveals connect to a smaller, A4-sized opening on the interior. Viewed from the inside, the resulting image appears as a random, "cut-out" fragment of a brick wall some 10 metres away, floating within and framed by the vast whiteness of the studio wall, which, apparently without thickness, is seemingly reduced to paper itself.

Kester Rattenbury

# Reading Sauerbruch Hutton

The books arrived by delivery, wrapped and sealed individually in translucent white paper. Both a dense neutral grey, with Sauerbruch Hutton's trademark lowercase font, the first book orange, the second baby blue. The page ends are colour-blocked, each side different: the first book yellow, green, pink; the second red, Yves Klein blue and a modernist acid greenish-yellow. They look like a pair but are actually an evolution: *archive 1* is paper-bound; *archive 2* cloth, with six coloured ribbon markers (mainly versions of gold) spaced through the book – as if to make up for their omission in the first volume. If there is any chance you have not noticed that Sauerbruch Hutton take enormous, intense care over everything they make, and how the user experiences it, these books would set you right.

A strange, minor benefit of Covid had been the unexpected access to books and requests to write about them. The rainbow flood of Sauerbruch Hutton's books was partly accidental: while eagerly grasping the chance to write about their work, I had to admit that I had never, to my knowledge, actually seen any of their buildings (except GSW, on the skyline, from the roof of the Reichstag, where it definitively edited and transfigured the view). The books began arriving. And at first, it seemed like they could be normal architectural books – if such things exist.

But insofar as these are typical, it's because they are consummate exemplars of something remarkable. Louisa and Matthias are clearly as adept in the eminent, surprising 500-year-old world of architectural books – that complex assembly of all sorts of images and text, designed to construct understanding of complicated, physical, extensively worked-out projects (built or unbuilt) that the reader could not otherwise visit – as they are in the world of building itself. Which is saying something.

As I write, under UK Lockdown #2 and #3, architectural books could indeed be regaining a significance that cheap air travel had eroded: their central, half-millennial role in sharing architectural knowledge, experience and imagination with those unable to visit the things themselves. And from within such constraints, it is startling how much they can do, by assembling and curating images and text on smallish bits of paper, nicely bound together.

The *archive* books are very comfortable with their tradition. They are essentially picture books, broadly chronological, with short, informative captions interspersed with longer texts – from Louisa and Matthias' lectures and publications – that set out the context and specifics of their work. If this is a catalogue raisonné, the reasoning is all in the work itself. As such, both volumes work as architecture books should: they allow you, with increasing knowledge, to assemble the exquisite, varied, always precise and carefully chosen drawings, photographs, plans, sections and renders (renders so convincing that you question their veracity) into a projected, partly understood sequence of built works.

The simplicity and clarity of the *archive* books are token of a considerable body of complex, resolved, disingenuously lucid, hard work. The acute selection of plans or sections; the ability to actually capture something about a project in the judicious choice of, say, two small images. The cartoon-like clarity of some of the early drawings – between Hergé and Vriesendorp? – are a million miles from sketches; they are graphic images that capture, simplify, select and represent the whole complex idea of a building, and present it to you as easily as though you were walking towards it. The texts, from republished papers and talks to the short captions, encapsulate the vast scope of work that these projects contain, from the history of Berlin to a working response to the climate emergency and a strong central value for human experience and beauty. And the books also include the most elegant (and informative) sustainability diagrams I've seen. This is all made available simply because they have already been through a mass of problems, options, possibilities and impossibilities for us. "If we can succeed in making something complex appear simple ... we regard that as a success," they say.

Reading this architecture fills me with awe. Sauerbruch Hutton are fractionally older than me, but much, much wiser. They seem to have been experienced, as well as rigorously experimental, from the start, preternaturally working with all the major issues of our time. They have taken on the memory and a humane sense of place; an early and profound engagement with environmental responsibilities; art. They always explore the uses of form, working both sides of what seemed (throughout most of this period) an internecine divide between straight and wiggly architecture. In one of their lecture texts, they randomly chose questions from the other, and gave long, reasoned answers to them. "Are curves better than corners?" Matthias asked. Louisa, naturally, values each – but, refreshingly, chooses. (Curves.)

The colour issue comes in early – and grows and grows, quickly assuming a fundamental role within their work. While the 1990–92 L House was "the first of our built projects where colour was applied as an actual building material", the H House was seen as "a large-format inhabited painting". Even the remarkable, immersive colour field qualities of these earlyish projects, where the experiences offered by the spaces are tangibly reshaped by the colours applied to them, does not begin to limit what they go on to do with them. It is not that everything is bright colours, but that colour of any kind has become an integral part and expressed dimension of the new reality they are devising.

And it immediately combines with planes, soft curves, glass and double-layered active and interactive environmental skins with complex composite patterns – all of which help to shape the world they are building and curating. This makes their projects luminescent, offset, warmer, cooler, bolder or more integrated. The rich use of colour, together with the complex environmental perimeters in which it increasingly becomes an active part, might at first look like a distinct corollary to their exquisite, near-minimal plans and sections, in which the messiness of everyday life and construction are somehow resolved and ordered into things of beauty. But dividing any aspect of Sauerbruch Hutton's work into separate components is surely a misinterpretation of how their refined and proactive assemblies work.

What the colour might actually do in each separate project is not constrained by the physical limitations of the building itself. It takes those projects further, into the human body, into the imagination, and also out into the city. Their use of large-scale urban photos, such as the famous ones of GSW across the Berlin skyline, show colour-heightened architecture that renders its settings more composed, rich, enjoyable – for everyone, not just their clients or occupants.

It extends to the optical games that all this can play, making for sheer delight. From the fabulous Michael Craig-Martin painting at the British Council in Berlin – transfigured and trebled by being painted on the ceiling, and given added Op Art, upside-down effects further surrealised by the curved framing of the bookshelves slithering past – to the soft curves and 36-toned spectrum of the Photonics Centre – cold hues to the north, warm ones to the south, with both the autumnal orangey reds and the fresh greens mingling with the groups of trees. Or the exquisite, playful and challenging *WYSIWYG* show, with its startling leaps of imagination and representation, built-in reality using mirrored tables, 3D specs and a shimmering palette of greens.

The building that set all this out on the international stage was the GSW redevelopment in Berlin. "The project took place in the magic moment after the fall of the Berlin Wall, when the potential future was stronger than all of the present," they say (p. 99). It aimed to "continue the story of the modernist city", taking on its limitations and problems, but still steering it towards a more ideal state. Specifically, it took on the emblematic role of its site in the south of Friedrichstadt, where the symbolic towers of East and West Berlin had until recently been staging an ideological face-off, by entirely reconfiguring the existing 1950s high-rise as part of a new conglomerate.

GSW's headline – its additional high-rise tower – thus acts as a working billboard for this new kind of redevelopment: both environmentally responsible, as well as embracing, recolouring, and making more lovely its urban context: "rejoining the two halves of the city". Its proclamatory and chic double-layered façade captures sunlight, controlled through solar shutters in various combinations of reds and pinks. This is operated by both the building management systems and individual choice, transfiguring an open convection façade protected by its wind roof into a "dynamic painting" that fuses occupancy with sustainability. Conceived in the short window before Berlin's ideology of "critical reconstruction" was imposed, it looks more modern, more lucid, more timeless and more visionary now than it did even then.

Because of the way the *archive* books are chronologically sequenced – larger schemes are shown first in their original design phase and then separately as a finished building upon completion – and because of the running series of reflective, as-found texts about them, the weaving and counterweaving of ideas through the work, the development, as the practice learns from its own work, becomes increasingly lucid. Ideas emerge and run on through the book as they do in practice: imagined, tested, picked up and explored again for other purposes, the arguments becoming ever more tangible.

And the growing sense of the extra demands that Sauerbruch Hutton make of themselves becomes increasingly clear. In their drawn-from-a-hat, Q&A lecture session, Matthias asks Louisa: "Art or Service?" She replies: "It's difficult to separate the ethical from the aesthetic ... we don't see this position as a contradiction ... Cannot the beautiful, the sensual, be sincere?" ... "Art *as* service" (p. 226). And unlike many who make similar claims, it's clear that they mean it.

So, by the end of book 1, reading Sauerbruch Hutton's work remotely, from hundreds of miles away, I could make confident bets about what the buildings are like. That they're wonderful. That you feel lapped by the colour – bathed in the landscape or thrilled by the city, warmed by the weather system that colour-field architecture makes. That they're clever, minimal. That there are moments that make you laugh, because they're so clever. That they feel simple, pleasurable – and only later do you realise how highly sophisticated and inventive they are; how much complexity has been resolved, say, through plan or section. That they're beautiful. That they do their job brilliantly.

But immediately on opening book 2 (a chronological continuum, but published ten years later), none of this is in question. We've moved to another level of conviction altogether. The practice is by now sizeable, doing many substantial projects in a (generally) recognisable appearance – but utterly without any sense of loss with regard to its specific, creative care for each building.

Something coherent has developed – is still developing – that is unique to them and that sets itself out for anyone to read. Something that is more than the sum of the parts: the generous, imaginative, informed and humane urban planning; beyond "just" the use of colour or form; beyond their active and holistic environmental agenda. Even beyond their demonstrable expertise in resolving complex spatial and social activities – including the clutter of everyday life – into almost sybaritically enjoyable places of all kinds, public and private, commercial and civic, all with a sense of equality of attention to any user.

It's that these various strands have fused into something extraordinary. The work seems to have become not just consummately resolved, generous, enjoyable buildings, but real artworks, too. Artworks made through the combination of intelligent environmental systems with remarkable, really precise colour work played out in three dimensions and engaging human experience. Even on the page, the buildings are striking, rich things that startle you: drawing you in from a distance or making you step up close, step away, or immerse yourself in them. By now, I was using the books – more than any other books I can remember – as an active surrogate for architectural experience itself.

This transfiguration – the sense that this architecture doesn't just reference artworks, it really *is* artwork – is first most evident in the presentation of the truly exquisite Brandhorst Museum. This is presaged by the excellent essay on museums, describing the everyday inspirational effects of a good museum: "A good museum will open up possibilities where few seemed to exist before. It will 'recharge your batteries'. Life will suddenly become possible again and will be full of unexpected potential" (p. 131). Just so.

But this sense grows and grows with the real, ongoing and often spectacular body of work, and the cumulative endeavour it comprises. The books actually begin to acquire the undoubted qualities of a Bridget Riley catalogue, with sequences of fascinating, often movingly beautiful mathematical and colour-formed works, developed at major urban scales and resolved in, and through, the realities of the worked-out buildings: plan and section, urban move and detail, circulation strategy and intimate place.

All of this pivoted, in my reader's mind, on the sophistication with which they have developed their sequences of entirely idiosyncratic layered, coloured, environmentally active façades – even though I resist seeing this as a separate thing. There is something about the City Dress project they showed at the 2006 Venice Biennale – with its bicoloured ribbons woven through padded silver silk – that reshaped my cognition of the range of dimensions in which this work is now operating.

And it was indeed a photo of Jessop West – the project described by City Dress – that startled me into this recognition. This is a real anaglyph of a building in which the offset, layer-separated colours, even in the photo, were so distinct that I took out my paper 3D specs to look at it. They worked, the photo leaping into startling new life: the silver façade panels bleached into 2D flat strips, luminous against the depth within the softer stripes of space between them. A woven, double-faced double space where the reflections of both the building itself and its neighbours unexpectedly stand out as a compositional layer in itself. Abstraction and reality are literally woven together, into the spatial experience that I was reading.

And from then on, I have been testing all of the photographs in this startling way. Of course, Sauerbruch Hutton *do* use anaglyphs; they used them in the wonderful *WYSIWYG* and other shows; they have a huge one hanging in their office. I even suspect that by now, they probably don't actually need the specs to see their own projects in this way.

So then that sense of the tough ongoing experiments in colour perception starts leaping off the pages. Look at the exquisite ADAC HQ building in Munich, its layered yellow frameworks oscillating against the skyline like a hallucinatory, inhabited anaglyph. Their work *obviously* includes that rigorous Rileyesque investigation of form, colour, patterning, perception, materials. And that investigation is inevitably intensified by its development in 3D. This is not just a sculptural move, but an exponential shift into a myriad dimensional realm, whose physical variables are always setting new challenges: the complex interaction of form, site, passive environmental design, structure, space, social activity (and viable economics, too). It's not only the physically complex, layered qualities of so many of the glazed façades, but also their environmental, technical and human operational demands. It's not only the artefacts themselves, but also the way they operate in the world: a multiplication of stringent demands – across scales, types and variables, from abstraction to working and occupied pragmatics.

Louisa's statement "Art *as* service" might sound simple – almost so as to elude notice. But as actually built, that endeavour is astounding, both in its levels of complexity and the success with which they have achieved it, across all the tasks that they have taken on.

This is absolutely *not* to say that the artistic qualities of their work diminish or overtake the sense of society, human life, practicalities, urban character – a criticism that used to be firmly levelled at so much high modernism at the time when they and I were students. No, it is to say that they clearly, demonstrably exemplify a practice that *does* actually practise what it preaches, by continuing modernism while directly addressing the problems it has generated: social, human, environmental. And by treating artworks not just as inspiration, but in the exigencies of considering buildings as artworks in themselves – public, shared artworks of the highest quality – which are treated as a working requirement, alongside all the other imperatives that they demonstrably manage to assimilate. They do everything that a really excellent practice does – to an extent most would deem impossible – and seem able to run a large organisation as though it were a small one.

In the period in which they and I have been working, it hasn't always been easy to see all this. Ironically, they have been masked, perhaps by the sheer determination of their sustained focus on the key aspects of our time through which architects can help shape and improve the world. Their long-standing commitment to the environmental agenda, their informed, intelligent appraisal and nourishing of the urban context, their overwhelming sense of human experience, their refined and experimental and tough uses of colour are all precise areas of engagement that are quintessential to their work. Meanwhile, in the wider world, these have become lazily applied tropes: slogans proclaimed rather than commitments undertaken. Even the very range of their work across various typologies (museums, offices, schools, warehouses, factories, beehives, flats) has – just perhaps – made their work seem more part of their time (which it undoubtedly is, as they say themselves [p. 273]) rather than a consummate, exemplary and (however quietly) game-changing force for good within it.

Perhaps even those exquisite, shimmering building skins have tended to *camouflage* their remarkable work, among generations of other architects who have also laid claim to colours, environmental intent, interest in art, the advantages of a range of forms – and who, for the most part, have done them far, far less well. With its ideal commitment to taking the concerns and possibilities of our age and using them to make something not just better, but of another and better order and quality altogether, their work is, for all its overt visibility, so well done as to achieve its own modesty. Which is perhaps why we do not always give it the full range of respect it most certainly deserves.

"It takes something like parents to turn a building into a being," they say (p. 204), and their commitment to their buildings, their output, is clearly of that nature. The "difficulties, insults, setbacks and disappointments" of everyday building parenting are never really on show. "Architecture is the only art that in all of its aspects is bound up with the lives of many people, not just one's own," they write (p. 230). So, if they praise teaching as a means of feeding back into "the network through which we all teach and learn", it's worth adding, as a teacher myself, that the primary way in which we teach and learn architecture is through looking at the best buildings that people have produced. Buildings whose generosity, commitment and many layers of achievement open a whole other dimension for us.

I have always admired their work, and loved the fragments I've seen in any shape, and yet it has literally taken me all this time to understand fully how utterly outstanding and richly wonderful it is. While Louisa and Matthias say that making something that is complex appear simple is a success, it does put the onus on the rest of us to pay attention to how they did it. To the extraordinary, transfigurative way in which things that may be merely tropes elsewhere – form, colour, expression, the nature of cities, the responsibilities to the wider environment, art in practice and experience, the quality of life for users – are here taken seriously and worked with, transformatively, time after time, rendered simple and full of pleasure. This is the most generous work. We should read what it tells us. And one day, if we ever get out of here, I'm looking forward to a real visit.

Lars Müller

# Architecture in Books

Paradoxically, despite all the media transformations, more books on architecture-related topics are being published today than ever before. Who is actually going to read them?

Over the past thirty years, the paradigm shift brought about by digitisation has also swept through architecture and the world of books, turning tried-and-tested rules upside down. Capitalist megalomania and the digital revolution are accelerating globalisation and making the book market more mainstream. The need for volume poses a threat to diversity in the publishing world. Output from independent publishers, valiantly holding their own in their particular niche, makes up only a tiny proportion of the market, as is also true of signature architecture considered in terms of the total volume of construction.

Without the benefit of lengthy hindsight, reflections on developments in the world of architecture over the three-decade period this publication addresses and on their significance for the future are tantamount to sandbox experiments, just like my musings concerning architecture books. Individually and collectively, erroneous conclusions are far from unlikely. However, mistakes in the realm of books never have the huge impact that flawed conclusions cause in architecture and urban planning.

To shed some light on the criteria informing my reflections, I would like to look back to a period 150 years ago. In the second half of the 19th century, technological and political processes accelerated, sparking enormous social and cultural upheavals. The Industrial Revolution and mass industrialisation went hand in hand with the advent of modern society, together with the urbanisation and class formation associated with this. The transformation from an agrarian to an industrial society unfolded without any institutionalised participation on the part of the emerging working class.

Throughout Europe, the proportion of city dwellers shot up rapidly, necessitating new construction, rectilinear city plans and the erection of large-scale blocks. In industrial building, reinforced concrete and steel-frame constructions able to enclose larger volumes prefigured technical, functional and stylistic facets of *Neues Bauen* (New Building). Society began to perceive architecture and engineering as promising, well-regarded professions. New schools and faculties were established to train young talent.

The enormous thirst for education invigorated the symbiosis between books and progress. Demand for publications on architecture, building and urban planning flourished and accounted for a large share of the market for non-fiction and reference books as they documented the rapid developments of the day. The leading figures in the profession also focused on teaching alongside their professional practice. They put their theories into words and drew on their own works to illustrate their ideas. Ernst Wasmuth opened his bookshop in Berlin in 1872. Although it was not the first, it would establish itself as the longest-standing bookshop for architectural literature in the German-speaking world and beyond, in conjunction with a specialised publishing house founded a little later. Revealing an early awareness of the significance and potential of the burgeoning medium of photography, the publisher employed in-house photographers as part of its support for the documentation of historical and contemporary architecture. Wasmuth published the first issue of the magazine *Der Städtebau* in 1904, followed in 1911 by the legendary portfolio *Ausgeführte Bauten und Entwürfe* by Frank Lloyd Wright. As is well documented, the architect funded the lavish execution of this work, also explicitly describing it as a tool for acquiring further business. Advertisements likewise provided financing for what were known as inauguration publications for specific buildings. In return, the publishers ensured widespread distribution. Wasmuth Verlag, for example, is known to have had a stand at an exhibition in St Louis, USA, in 1904.

The rapid developments in construction technology and the discourse about attitudes and styles generated an upturn in books on architecture and a whole host of other areas. With the Secession movements in Vienna (1897) and elsewhere in the late 1890s, and the founding of the Werkbund (1907), this new dawn spilled over into the fine arts and the applied arts, too, with their insights and achievements rapidly being transposed into the medium of the book. By this time, the printing trade had adapted to increasingly large print runs, and while books did not necessarily become cheap, they remained affordable for professionals who were keen to keep abreast of new developments.

Although the period from the 1890s until the outbreak of war in Europe in 1914 saw the rapid publication of a number of books that would in retrospect prove relevant for architectural historiography, their number increased even further after the war as a result of the activism unleashed in European society by the recent upheavals. In art, new -isms came thick and fast, while associations and institutions founded in response to the need for renewal viewed the book as the appropriate medium for the dissemination of their views and goals.

*Neues Bauen, die Neue Wohnung* (The New Apartment), every conceivable innovation or argument was first circulated on paper during this era – in the form of leaflets, pamphlets, magazines or books. Political topics found an audience, too, and sparked debate on subjects such as land ownership or housing for low-income groups. The reference book, originally aimed at professionals, shed its elitist arrogance and the paperback made political literature available for the mass market.

*Neue Typografie* (New Typography) and a novel use of language, conceived for concise, efficient statements, often with a certain propagandistic impetus, began to appear in non-fiction and reference books. Book design experimented with new typefaces and unprecedented layouts.

Successful architects began to see writing and publishing books as an inseparable part of their professional identity. Publishing also became an arena in which architects competed for attention, recognition and commissions. In addition, the profession of independent editor became established, drawing on expertise and a grasp of the broader context to compile and organise information in order to render it comprehensible within the structure of the book. Journalists provided copy for magazines on art, architecture and home interiors, paving the way for a market boom and fostering exchanges between modern movements in Europe. Addressing how

National Socialism stymied this revival in 1933 would go beyond the scope of this essay.

Instead, I would like to highlight an exemplary publishing project. In 1929, the young architects Willy Boesiger (1904–1990) and Oscar Gregory Stonorov (1905–1970), who had both briefly worked at 35 rue de Sèvres in Paris, approached Le Corbusier together with Zurich publisher Hans Girsberger (1898–1982) to propose a monograph on the buildings he had designed and realised since 1910.

Having previously published numerous books that he had written and edited himself, Le Corbusier agreed to the project and shared decision-making authority and oversight of the content with the editors and the publisher, who were committed to depicting and presenting this objectively. They had no idea that the project would lead to more than 30 years of collaboration and loyal friendship. Volume 7 in the series was being printed when Le Corbusier died in 1965. All the volumes adhered to the original principles for the books' structure and layout, including the landscape format, still unusual in 1929, which Le Corbusier had explicitly requested.

The initiative taken by those young men resulted in a unique body of work bringing together many ideals that, in my opinion, guide a publisher. As an attentive observer in the midst of his Zurich friends, Hans Girsberger followed up on a number of fleetingly mentioned ideas and initiated projects that gave rise to one of the most important architectural publishing programmes of that period by the Verlag für Architektur and, later, Artemis Verlag.* After the Second World War, Girsberger and others invoked the principles of early modernism and accompanied Europe's reconstruction through their publications. The original intentions of planners and architects were often undermined and distorted by the might of capital, the building boom and the economic miracle. Publications presenting unrealised architectural and urban planning projects bear witness to that. Architects were instrumentalised to implement strategies obsessed with growth. To this day, a small but impressively influential minority in the profession pushes back against this phenomenon, realising exemplary new work and presenting their convictions and projects thanks to like-minded publishing houses.

## Tempi passati

A century on, the attitude adopted by Wasmuth, Girsberger and other publishers in the book trade has given way to the pragmatic imperatives of a service-oriented business. Nowadays, the range of books on offer is dominated by a shocking number of trivial best-of compilations and coffee-table books. Discourse on architectural and planning issues is restricted to a niche publishing market.

In the mid-1980s, the digital realm was lauded as the promised land. Echoing the situation a century earlier, design-related fields were promptly pervaded by an enthusiasm for the new, and soon provided the first examples of how the new technology would alter processes and outcomes in architecture and design. In the first instance, however, the promise of a new aesthetic did not materialise. Rationalisation of processes took precedence and served to justify the investments made. It was not until computer capacity became more widely available in the 1990s that the opportunity to add a new formal language to the modernist canon arose, with amorphous forms incorporated into complex architectural designs.

Books underwent a similar evolution. The digital transformation filtered through into book design, as manifested in frivolous typography without concern for legibility or long-established golden rules. Nonetheless, the digital world could not do away with the physical parameters that define books. They retained their shape and their heft.

From the mid-1990s, the internet rapidly developed into a mass medium and transformed the public's expectations and habits. Search engines linked information in real time. The book, a manifesto for democratised knowledge a hundred years earlier, came under pressure due to free content made available on new platforms promoting the self-same promise. The apparent advantage was access to precisely the information required, albeit often in a fragmentary form.

Non-fiction and reference books lost ground, while literature was consumed in insubstantial digital formats. With the rise of social media, interpersonal communication also took its leave of analogue reality. Handwriting has atrophied, as has vocabulary and language. In the light of such laments, books were expected to disappear until just recently. And yet the power of the internet has never managed to compensate for its loss of editorial diligence.

Whereas printed books were once the exclusive source of information, they are now jockeying for position in a convergent media landscape. Euphoria about the digital realm has subsided and the pros and cons of various media are being weighed up. In this context, it has transpired that the internet is well suited to architectural subject matter, documenting ongoing processes and presenting up-to-date lists and catalogues of work that – in the world of print – are merely dutiful appendices and often outdated even before publication. Digital presentations also draw on moving and animated images to explain and entertain.

Against this background, the typology of the architectural book has changed. The architectural monograph has lost its professional audience. It still holds its own on the shelves, fanning the flames of the star cult and supplying an eclectic audience with trite texts written to order and accompanied by sleek and shiny photographs. The coffee-table book is the dominant species. Emulating the luxury and fashion market, it showcases visions of dream destinations all over the world, the most beautiful hotels, the most spacious villas or aspirational interiors for glossy lifestyle magazines. In addition, handbooks on ecology and innovations in architectural technology have taken root as "must-have" works that rapidly become obsolete in the face of technological change, giving the book market regular boosts thanks to their fast obsolescence.

In all, this would be a bleak outlook, were it not for the handful of publishers who, in conjunction with figures from research, development and practice, hold fast to their ideals against the grain of popular trends. With a critical eye and a keen sense for the bigger picture, they monitor social, political and cultural developments that call for rapid identification, response and adaption, in particular among design-related disciplines.

In the academic context, the book is still the key medium, albeit for a dwindling audience. This is evident in a growing number of theoretical texts on architecture and planning that use the book as a format to stimulate contemporary discourse with their arguments. The *instrument* of the theoretical text soon becomes a *document* of engagement with its time and a point of reference for further research. There is no sign of any digital substitute for this duality.

Those authors are not practising architects, as was the case in the early and mid-20th century, but are instead mostly intellectuals from closely related disciplines. When it comes to disseminating their views, architects prefer the time-saving interview format to their own committed writing. Only a few escape this dilemma and follow Le Corbusier's example. They periodically present the results of their explorations and practice as a complete collection in book form, relying on expressing themselves in their own language. The monograph also continues to hold its own as an enduring repository in the sense of a collection that brings together a completed body of work, with its own value and demonstrable impact. Depicting an oeuvre in book form to document ongoing projects is useful only if the work can serve as an example to demonstrate an idea or insight that forms the underlying premise. It is a demanding and costly genus, just as it was in the days of the pioneers.

From the small publisher's perspective, much has changed for the worse over the past few decades. Claims that advertising revenue would keep digital information free of charge in the long run has proved to be a neoliberal fallacy. However, that assumption has exerted enormous price pressure on the book as a medium. Retailers outdo each other in slashing prices, and publishers are being forced to cut editorial input. The much-vaunted democratic principle of book-based culture, which asserts that the costs and benefits of books should be shared among as many readers as possible, now seems outdated.

With steadfast defiance and common sense, our slim niche can tap into the advantages of digital communication to reach a larger, global audience and enable it to participate in our universal content. That is how the analogue book, with all its virtues, will be able to stand its ground in the virtual realm. Hope is the last thing we lose.

*   Hans Girsberger became a role model for my own publishing activity thanks to a note in the preface to the reprint of Alfred Roth's *Die Neue Architektur/La Nouvelle Architecture/The New Architecture* (1939/1959), which led me to conclude optimistically that a publisher is, above all else, an initiator and enabler and the spiritus rector of ambitious book projects. Girsberger: "I remember [...] how we – my friend, the young architect Alfred Roth, and I, the young publisher just starting out – were toying with all kinds of publishing plans as we talked enthusiastically on the way home from the coffee house around midnight in the summer of 1938, and then, bursting with high spirits, decided to create a unique work on architecture that would meet the highest standards and be aimed at international architects." And that is precisely what they did.

## Biographies

**Thomas Auer** (*1965, Spaichingen) is an engineer and Professor of Building Technology and Climate Responsive Design at the Technical University of Munich, and a partner at Transsolar Energietechnik. Both his research and his consultancy work with renowned architectural firms worldwide focus on environmental quality, innovative design and robustness in the context of a sustainable transformation of the built environment. Auer is a member of the Convention of Baukultur and Berlin's Akademie der Künste.

**Barry Bergdoll** (*1955, Chester) is Meyer Schapiro Professor of Art History and Archaeology at Columbia University, where he gained his PhD in 1986. He was chief curator of architecture and design at MoMA, New York, from 2007 to 2014. Exhibitions he curated there include *Mies in Berlin* (2001, with Terence Riley), and *Bauhaus 1919–1933: Workshops for Modernity* (2009–10). Bergdoll has written on K. F. Schinkel, Marcel Breuer, Frank Lloyd Wright and on aspects of 19th-century French architecture.

**Marco Biscione** (*1958, Rome) trained as an anthropologist at the University of Rome and the London School of Economics. After almost two decades as curator at the Museo Nazionale Preistorico Etnografico in Rome, he became a national expert in culture at the European Commission and later at the Council of Europe. Back in Italy, he served as director of the Civic Museums of Udine, of the Museo d'Arte Orientale in Turin and, more recently, of M9 – Museum of the 20th Century, in Venice-Mestre.

**Jean-Louis Cohen** (*1949, Paris) is an architect and a historian. He has held the Chair for the History of Architecture at New York University's Institute of Fine Arts since 1993. His many books include *France. Modern Architectures in History* (2015), *Le Corbusier: An Atlas of Modern Landscapes* (2013) and *The Future of Architecture. Since 1889* (2012). Cohen has curated numerous exhibitions, including at the Centre Georges Pompidou, the Canadian Centre for Architecture (CCA) and MoMA, New York.

**Sir Peter Cook** (*1936, Southend-on-Sea) is an architect and a writer. He co-founded Archigram in the 1960s, taught at the Architectural Association (1964–90), was a professor at the Städelschule in Frankfurt (1984–2009), a Bartlett Professor and Chair (1990–2006) and a RIBA Royal Gold Medallist (jointly with Archigram) in 2002. He was knighted for his services to architecture and teaching in 2007. His buildings include the Kunsthaus Graz (with Colin Fournier) and the Law Faculty of Vienna's Business and Economics University (with Gavin Robotham).

**Kristin Feireiss** (*1942, Berlin) is an architectural curator, author and publisher. In 1980, she co-founded the first private architecture gallery in Europe: the Berlin-based Aedes Architecture Forum – and has been its director ever since, from 1994 together with Hans-Jürgen Commerell. From 1996–2001, she was director of the Netherlands Architecture Institute in Rotterdam, and in 1996 and 2000 served as commissioner of the Dutch Pavilion at the Venice Biennale of Architecture. Feireiss is a former jury member of the Pritzker Architecture Prize.

**Angelika Fitz** (*1967, Hohenems) directs the Architekturzentrum Wien (AZW). Prior to this, she worked internationally as a curator, writer and consultant in the fields of architecture and urbanism. Recent exhibitions and publications include *We-Traders. Swapping Crisis for City* (2013–15), *Actopolis* (2015–17) and, together with the AZW, *Downtown Denise Scott Brown* (2018). In 2019, Fitz and Elke Krasny co-curated the exhibition *Critical Care. Architecture for a Broken Planet.*

**Kurt W. Forster** (*1935, Zurich) has held professorships at Stanford University, M.I.T., the ETH Zurich, the Bauhaus University in Weimar and the universities of Yale and Princeton. He has organised architecture exhibitions on K. F. Schinkel, Carlo Scarpa and Herzog & de Meuron, and in 2004 directed the 9th Venice Biennale of Architecture. Forster's publications include *Karl Friedrich Schinkel. A Meander through His Life and Work* (2018) and *Aby Warburgs Kulturwissenschaft. Ein Blick in die Abgründe der Bilder* (2018).

**Adrian Forty** (*1948, Oxford) is Emeritus Professor of Architectural History at the Bartlett School of Architecture, University College London. He is the author of *Objects of Desire: Design and Society, 1750–1980* (1986), *Words and Buildings: A Vocabulary of Modern Architecture* (2000) and *Concrete and Culture: a Material History* (2012). Forty was president of the European Architectural History Network from 2010 to 2014 and is currently Honorary Curator of Architecture at the Royal Academy, London.

**Florian Heilmeyer** (*1974, Tübingen) is a writer, curator, historian and critic with a focus on architecture and the city. He is currently writing a book about contemporary public architecture in Flanders (together with the Flanders Architecture Institute) and a monograph on Sauerbruch Hutton's Experimenta building. As a freelancer, he is also a regular contributor to architectural publications such as *BauNetz, Baumeister, Metropolis Magazine* and *Werk, Bauen + Wohnen.* Heilmeyer lives in Berlin.

**Louisa Hutton** (*1957, Norwich) is an architect and co-founder of Sauerbruch Hutton. She has taught at the AA, London, Harvard GSD and the University of Virginia, and lectures, participates in juries and contributes to conferences worldwide. She is an Honorary Fellow of the AIA, a member of the Freie Akademie der Künste in Hamburg and a Royal Academician of the Royal Academy of Arts in London, where she currently chairs the Architecture Committee. Hutton was awarded an OBE in 2015.

**Ola Kolehmainen** (*1964, Helsinki) is an artist who works exclusively in the medium of photography. Known for capturing architectural space in a way that oscillates between 2D and 3D readings, he has lately redirected his attention from 20th- and 21st-century works to sacred historical monuments, classical art museums and institutional photographic archives. His work has been displayed in numerous group and monographic exhibitions worldwide. Kohlemainen lives and works in Berlin.

**Kieran Long** (*1977, Lyndhurst) is a journalist and curator who, since 2017, has directed ArkDes, the Swedish Centre for Architecture and Design in Stockholm. He established the department of Design, Architecture and Digital at the Victoria and Albert Museum in London in 2013–14 and served as its keeper until 2017. Before becoming assistant director to David Chipperfield's curatorial team at the 2012 Venice Biennale of Architecture, Long was an architecture critic and editor, teacher and TV presenter.

**Ijoma Mangold** (*1971, Heidelberg) studied literature and philosophy in Munich and Bologna in the 1990s. After working for the *Berliner Zeitung* and the *Süddeutsche Zeitung,* he joined *Die Zeit* in 2009, where he headed the literature section from 2013 to 2018. He is currently the Zeit correspondent for cultural policy. Mangold received the Berlin Prize for Literary Criticism in 2007. His autobiography, *Das deutsche Krokodil – Meine Geschichte*, was published in 2017. Mangold lives in Berlin.

**Gerhard Matzig** (*1963, Deggendorf) studied political science, law and architecture in Bochum, Passau and Munich, graduating in 1993. After working as a freelance journalist, he joined the editorial staff of the *Süddeutsche Zeitung* in 1997, where he has been senior editor since 2001. The Munich-based author has won numerous awards for his reviews and essays and has published several books. Matzig has taught architectural theory as a visiting professor in Vienna and Lübeck, and writes on architecture, urbanism and design.

**Mohsen Mostafavi** (*1954, Isfahan) is an architect and educator. He served as dean of Harvard GSD and is the Alexander and Victoria Wiley Professor of Design and Harvard University Distinguished Service Professor. His work focuses on processes of urbanisation and on the interface between technology and aesthetics. He has written and co-authored numerous books. Mostafavi is a consultant on a number of architectural and urban projects, including the Future of the American City Project: Miami. He also heads a research project on Japanese urbanism.

**Lars Müller** (*1955, Oslo) trained as a graphic designer. He published his first book in 1983 and has produced some 800 titles to date – ranging from typography and design to art, photography and architecture. A passionate educator, he has taught at various universities in Switzerland and abroad, including Harvard GSD from 2009 to 2017 and as Regents' Professor at UCLA in 2019. Müller frequently serves on academic and competition juries and has been based in Switzerland since 1963.

**Anh-Linh Ngo** (*1974, Kon Tum) is co-publisher and editor-in-chief of *ARCH+*. He studied architecture at RWTH Aachen University and has been a publicist and curator since 2004. He co-curated the exhibitions *An Atlas of Commoning* at Kunstraum Bethanien in Berlin (2018) and *1989–2019: Politics of Space in the New Berlin* at Neuer Berliner Kunstverein (2019). Ngo is a co-founder of the international initiative *projekt bauhaus.* In 2020, *ARCH+* was awarded the Berlin Art Prize in the architecture section by the Akademie der Künste.

**Eric Parry** (*1952, Kuwait City) studied architecture throughout the 1970s at Newcastle University and in London at the Royal College of Art and the Architectural Association. He founded Eric Parry Architects in 1983 and was appointed a lecturer in architecture at the University of Cambridge, where he taught for fourteen years. Parry has served on the Mayor of London's design advisory panel, was elected a Royal Academician in 2006, and in 2012 received an honorary degree of Doctor of Arts from the University of Bath.

**Kester Rattenbury** (*1961, Taunton) is an architectural writer, teacher and professor at the University of Westminster in London, with a PhD on architectural coverage in the UK national press. She set up the research group Experimental Practice in 2003, with its Archigram Archival Project and Supercrit series. Key publications include *This Is Not Architecture* (2002) on architectural media, *The Wessex Project* on Thomas Hardy (2018), as well as works on Cedric Price, O'Donnell + Tuomey and practice-based research.

**Karin Sander** (\*1957, Bensberg) is a conceptual artist who lives and works in Berlin and Zurich. In her art, she questions the structural, social and historical contexts of existing situations and spaces, using a range of media to create new ways of seeing and experiencing them. Her works have been presented in solo exhibitions and at biennales throughout the world and are to be found in the public collections of many countries. Since 2007, Sander has held the chair for Architecture and Art at the ETH Zurich.

**Matthias Sauerbruch** (\*1955, Constance) is an architect and founding director of Sauerbruch Hutton. He taught at the AA, London, and has held professorships at the TU Berlin, the SAbK Stuttgart, Harvard GSD and the University of Virginia. He contributes to juries and conferences worldwide and is a founding member of the German Sustainable Building Council. Sauerbruch is the director of architecture at the Akademie der Künste in Berlin and an Honorary Fellow of the American Institute of Architects.

**Veronica Simpson** (\*1962, Blyth) is a London-based visual arts writer and editor with nearly three decades' experience in seeking out and appraising the most interesting cultural, social and aesthetic evolutions in design, architecture and art. With a masters in environmental psychology, she puts the human experience first, uncovering and articulating the mechanisms by which design, art and architecture can make a difference. Simpson is a regular contributor to a range of specialist publications.

**Philip Ursprung** (\*1963, Baltimore) is a Swiss art historian. He has been Professor of the History of Art and Architecture at the ETH Zurich since 2011. He studied in Geneva, Vienna and Berlin and has also taught at the Universität der Künste Berlin, Columbia and Cornell universities, New York, as well as the University of Zurich. He is editor of *Herzog & de Meuron: Natural History* (2002) and author of *Allan Kaprow, Robert Smithson, and the Limits to Art* (2013). Ursprung's most recent book is *Joseph Beuys: Kunst Kapital Revolution* (2021).

**Dirk van den Heuvel** (\*1968, Apeldoorn) is an architect, editor and curator who holds the chair of Architecture and Dwelling at the TU Delft. He co-founded and heads the Jaap Bakema Study Centre at Het Nieuwe Instituut in Rotterdam. He received a Richard Rogers Fellowship from Harvard University GSD in 2017 and was a visiting scholar at Monash University, Melbourne, in 2019. Recent publications include *Habitat: Ecology Thinking in Architecture* (2020) and *Art on Display 1949-69* (2019).

**Georg Vrachliotis** (\*1977, Berlin) is Professor of Theory of Architecture and Digital Culture at the TU Delft. He was dean of Karlsruhe's KIT Faculty of Architecture and Chair of Architecture Theory there from 2014 to 2020. Vrachliotis studied architecture in Berlin and gained his PhD at the ETH Zurich. His research, exhibitions and publications focus on architecture, media and technology in the 20th and 21st centuries. Among the exhibitions he has curated is *Models, Media and Methods. Frei Otto's Architectural Research* (2020).

**Mark Wigley** (\*1956, Palmerston North) is Professor and Dean Emeritus at Columbia University's Graduate School of Architecture. As an architectural historian, theorist and critic, he explores the intersection of architecture, art, philosophy, culture and technology. Recent publications include *Konrad Wachsmann's Television: Post-Architectural Transmissions* (2020) and *Cutting Matta-Clark: The Anarchitecture Investigation* (2018). Wigley has curated exhibitions in New York, Montreal, Rotterdam, Istanbul and Shanghai.

# 164

**the turn of the century**
A Reader about Architecture in Europe 1990–2020

Edited by Matthias Sauerbruch and Louisa Hutton
Editorial assistance: Isabelle Hartmann
Translations from the German and Italian: Helen Ferguson
Translation from the French: Christian Hubert / Helen Ferguson
Copy-editing and proof-reading: Danko Szabó
Coordination: Maya Rüegg
Design: Heimann + Schwantes, Berlin
Lithography: prints professional, Berlin
Printing and binding: DZA Druckerei zu Altenburg

Lars Müller Publishers is supported by the Swiss Federal
Office of Culture with a structural contribution for the years
2021–2024.

Lars Müller Publishers, Zurich, Switzerland
www.lars-mueller-publishers.com

Distributed in North America by ARTBOOK | D.A.P.
www.artbook.com

ISBN 978-3-03778-674-1
Printed in Germany

Titles on Sauerbruch Hutton by Lars Müller Publishers:

Sauerbruch Hutton Archive
2006, ISBN 978-3-03778-083-1

Sauerbruch Hutton Archive 2
2016, ISBN 978-3-03778-389-4